AFTER *STRANGE FRUIT*

AFTER
STRANGE FRUIT

Changing Literary Taste
in post—World War II Boston

P. Albert Duhamel
Philomatheia Professor Boston College

Lectures Delivered for the
National Endowment for the Humanities
Boston Public Library
Learning Library Program

Boston, Trustees of the Public Library
of the City of Boston, 1980

Library of Congress Cataloging in Publication Data

Duhamel, Pierre Albert, 1920-
After *Strange Fruit.*

(Publication—National Endowment for the Humanities Learning
Library Program, Boston Public Library; no. 10)
"Originally delivered as a series of lectures at the Boston Public Library
in the fall of 1976."
  1. Books and reading—Massachusetts—Boston—Addresses, essays,
lectures. 2. Censorship—Massachusetts—Boston—Addresses, essays,
lectures. 3. Boston —Intellectual life—Addresses, essays, lectures. 4.
American literature—20th century—History and criticism—Addresses,
essays, lectures.
  I. Boston. Public Library. II. Title.

Library of Congress Cataloging in Publication Data

III. Series: Boston. Public Library. National Endowment for the
Humanities Learning Library Program. Publication—National
Endowment for the Humanities Learning Library Program, Boston
Public Library; 10. Z1003.3.M4D83   028'.9   79-21899
ISBN 0-89073-063-6

Contents

Introduction

The eight chapters in this book were originally delivered as a series of lectures at the Boston Public Library in the fall of 1976 as part of a continuing program supported by the National Endowment for the Humanities which had designated the Boston library as a "learning library" and contributed to its mission of providing the citizens of Boston with opportunities for education and self-development in cultural subjects of interest to them.

Several months before, Philip McNiff, director of the Boston Public Library, had encouraged me to develop some comments I had been making on changes in literary taste in post–World War II Boston. He thought he had just the right audience to test or applaud my observations. So I pulled together materials on the novel, drama, and poetry that I thought might be of particular interest to Bostonians and arranged them in a progression that was intended not only to provide some historical orientation in the evaluation of obvious changes but also some encouragement and guidance in the formation of personal critical positions. Thus the first lecture was heavily historical in content, tracing the series of legal decisions which had determined what Bostonians could read, and the last lecture was rather pedagogical and exhortatory, urging the regular library users to become critical, independent readers.

Mr. McNiff knew his audience. They proved interesting, informed, and challenging. At each of the lectures, with Paul M. Wright, head of the Learning Library Program, supervising all the many details, we distributed suggested reading lists for the next session and all sorts of materials—paragraphs from books, reviews of books, poems, editorials—intended to provoke discussion. Several times members of the audience supplied from their own experiences memories of show openings, author lectures, and political squabbles that supplemented the written historical record we were discussing.

To provide the detail and color these audiences expected, we were fortunate in securing as guest lecturers and discussion leaders some Bostonians who had been intimate observers and participants in the development of Boston's cultural life for the previous thirty years. Elliot Norton, drama critic of the *Boston Herald American,* gave a talk on the Boston theater and went on to give a complete series on the subject the following spring which has already appeared in book form, *Broadway Down East.* John Galvin, author of several studies on Boston political figures, spoke on the Boston political novel. Ruth Whitman, poet and teacher of poetry around Boston for many years, reviewed the recent poetry of many local poets she knew well. Richard McDonough, an editor at Little, Brown and close observer of Boston reading habits for many years, took the audience through the changes in the social novel that he thought had been particularly important and, like all the guest lecturers, fielded questions afterward.

1

From the *Boston Evening Transcript* to the *Boston Phoenix*

On Sunday night, March 11, 1945, Abraham Isenstadt, seated in the front row of a large audience assembled at Boston's John Hancock Hall for a lecture on race problems in the South, must have entertained some ironic reflections on the justice of the proceedings. The lecture, part of a long-established series widely known from the location where the meetings were ordinarily held as the Ford Hall Forum Series, had been moved from the usual hall on Boylston Street to the much larger auditorium because the speaker, Miss Lillian Smith, had suddenly become a national celebrity. Her recently published novel, *Strange Fruit,* had just been banned in Boston.

Until the local bookstores, complying with a request made by Police Commissioner Thomas F. Sullivan late in February, had removed *Strange Fruit* from public sale, Miss Smith had escaped public notice working as an editor throughout the South and publishing some undistinguished fiction. But now, the forty-eight-year-old stately, some thought "schoolmistressy," figure commanded the attention of the crowd as a controversial author. She stuck to her subject, race problems in the South, and did not discuss the banning of her book in Boston. When she had completed her talk, members of the audience came up and asked her to autograph copies of her book, which could no longer be purchased in Boston stores.

Abraham Isenstadt had to wonder why there were no police around impounding those copies of *Strange Fruit* for, just the week before, he had been fined for selling a copy to Bernard De Voto, widely known for his monthly column in *Harper's* wherein he regularly discussed new books. A Harvard Square bookseller, Isenstadt had been taken to court because he had defied a curious arrangement which had been first worked out, way back in 1913, between the Boston Watch and Ward Society and the Boston Board of Retail Book Merchants whereby any book which the watchers found offensive the retailers would then refuse to sell and the police would prosecute anyone who failed to comply.

Strange Fruit had been in the bookstores for almost a year before it had been noticed and then become controversial in Boston, and Isenstadt got in trouble for selling a copy. Edward Weeks, editor of the *Atlantic Monthly,* had reviewed it along with other recently published novels in his monthly column, "The Atlantic Bookshelf," for May 1944 (vol. 173, p. 127) warning that it was "like a hand grenade tossed into a tea party" because it "takes the reader beneath the surface of a little Southern town and there discusses frankly, in human terms and with the high voltage of emotion, themes which it is polite not to discuss—miscegenation, abortion, and white supremacy."

It was not the themes which would make the novel objectionable, but, as Weeks anticipated, some words, and he called attention to the existence of some "scenes so coarse in word and implication that they are bound to offend." He went on to conclude: "But despite the shock that is here, I find nothing in the novel that is pornographic."

Some Bostonian presumably did for, according to a report published in the *Boston Record American* on March 21, 1945, Police Commissioner Thomas F. Sullivan received, some time in February of that year, a call from an unidentified person complaining that he had just bought a copy of *Strange Fruit* which contained some words in print that he thought were never to be found in print. The commissioner must have investigated the matter further for he is quoted as having requested the Board of Retail Book Merchants to withdraw the book because of "certain indecent passages" which he considered "the boldest" he had ever seen in reference to sex relations. The newspaper report noted that the book dealt with miscegenation but that it had not been objected to because of its subject matter.

In the South it had. The *Atlantic Monthly* for August 1944 (vol. 174, p. 129) reprints a letter from Thomas Harrold of Macon, Georgia, who describes himself as "having been reared in a small South Georgia county-seat and having practiced medicine for twenty years in one of the larger cities of the state." With that background as his authority, he gives it as his opinion that "miscegenation is no longer a problem of any importance in this state." He concludes with an expression of sorrow that the book was written because it gives what seems to him "a wholly unjustified and fictitious picture of race relations in Georgia and the South." He agrees with Weeks's review that "the pornographic angle is unimportant" and that "the four-letter words could have been omitted easily enough," so some Southern reaction to the book was completely at odds with the official Bostonian position.

When the political arrangement invoked to ban *Strange Fruit* had first been worked out between the Watch and Ward Society and the Board of Retail Book Merchants back in 1913, the Boston police commissioner was not then involved as he had become by 1945. In the beginning the Watch and Ward Society and the retail booksellers had created a joint committee which undertook to monitor questionable volumes. Whenever this committee agreed that some book offended their sense of taste or violated their definition of obscenity, they would warn their booksellers, who would refuse to stock the books, and notify the newspapers, who would neither advertise nor review the book. District attorneys would prosecute any bookseller who decided to sell the book anyway, and judges tended to convict dealers who set themselves up against the community.

This was the system in operation in 1925 when Theodore Dreiser's *American Tragedy* was banned. Donald Friede, a partner in the New York publishing house of Boni and Liveright, came to Boston to precipitate a test case and had himself arrested for selling a copy of the book to a police lieutenant. Convicted in a municipal court, he carried the case all the way to the supreme court of the commonwealth where Judge Pierce, rendering a decision reaffirming the guilty decisions of the lower courts had this to say: "Even assuming real literary excellence, artistic worth and an impelling moral lesson to the story, there is nothing essential to the history of the life of its principal character that would be lost if these passages were omitted which the jury found were obscene, indecent and manifestly tending to corrupt the morals of youth."

Thus the literary taste and morals of the greater Boston community were protected down through 1926 when Henry L. Mencken contrived to have himself arrested for selling to J. Frank Chase, then secretary of the Watch and Ward Society, a copy of the April issue of the *American Mercury* magazine which had been banned in Boston because it contained a story, "Hatrack," by Herbert Asbury, about a prostitute, which had been considered offensive by the joint committee. The establishment was surprised when Judge James D. Parmenter ruled that the magazine should not have been banned in Boston.

Emboldened by the decision, Mencken and the *Mercury* sued for an injunction against further interference by the Watch and Ward Society with the sale of their magazine and were delighted when Judge James M. Morton, Jr., of the district court warned the society that they were securing "their influence, not by voluntary acquiescence in their opinions by the trade in question, but by the coercion and intimidation of that trade, through fear of prosecution if the defendants' views are disregarded." In my judgment, he concluded, "this is clearly illegal."

The Watch and Ward Society was stunned for they were on notice that, continuing with their present arrangement, they might be sued for coercion and restraint of trade. It was then that they and the booksellers turned to the superintendent of police and the district attorney of Suffolk County for guidance, and these two officials now came to occupy a central position in the banning of books. They proved to be far less tolerant than the Watch and Ward Society for in March 1927 alone some nine novels were banned.

In April 1927, District Attorney William J. Foley decided that Sinclair Lewis's new novel about sham religious sects and clerical hypocrises, *Elmer Gantry,* was objectionable and set in motion the machinery to keep it out of the bookstores. Richard Fuller, manager of the Old Corner Bookstore, was suddenly caught with a display window full of the books. Since Lewis had just won the Pulitzer Prize for Literature and then declined the honor, Fuller had jumped the gun to promote the currently controversial author feeling sure he would sell many copies of the new title with his store-window promotion. He was so anxious to comply with the surprise order that he rushed all the copies of *Elmer Gantry* out of the window and substituted other titles so fast that he forgot to remove a picture of Lewis which remained behind to puzzle browsers.

This was the atmosphere in which books published in 1927 were received in Boston. In that first year after the court decision which led to a substitute of police censorship for the previous monitoring of the Watch and Ward Society, sixty to a hundred books—estimates vary—were banned. Among them were Conrad Aiken's *Blue Voyage,* John Dos Passos's *Manhattan Transfer,* Ernest Hemingway's *The Sun Also Rises,* and William Faulkner's *Mosquitoes*—all now commonly recognized as significant works of American literature.

Through those years Boston was not without a public forum for the discussion of new books. The *Boston Evening Transcript* had been publishing a regular book review section since 1922. At least two full pages, it appeared in the Saturday evening edition of the paper, the most extensive edition, right next to "Notes and Queries," a regular genealogical feature tracing the ancestries of prominent Boston families, the most popular item in the entire paper.

In the late 1920s, the *Evening Transcript* was still a powerful tastemaker in Boston. Its income in those days was still impressive especially from the so-called tombstone advertisements which were regularly placed in the paper to notify trust officers of the issue of new securities. Revenue began to fall off during the Depression thirties when store advertising declined and circulation dropped way off. When the *Transcript* finally folded, on April 30, 1941, its circulation was probably down to 30,000, though it claimed some 40,000.

Some idea of the values which governed the editorial policies of the paper may be gathered from its last editorial. It began, "here, with No. 101, Volume CXII, the *Boston Evening Transcript* closes its career of something over a century." It then went on to quote from a poem by Thackeray and to recall, as expressive of the spirit of the disappearing paper, several paragraphs from an Easter editorial that had appeared just a fortnight before. The editorial had called for a reaffirmation of a belief in the faith which had animated the paper from its beginning. "The great question of our time is whether we have the courage to live that faith. For Christianity is a way of living, not a theological doctrine. The laws of love mean sacrifice and discipline. Applied Christianity is a prerequisite to the only kind of social unity that can bring order from the present chaos."

To round out the picture of what the paper had always stood for, this last editorial of the *Transcript* concluded by reprinting its first, which had appeared on July 24, 1830. It had then spelled out its intended posture with statements like these: "We belong to the sect called Protestant Episcopalian: we feel that our opinions are liberal; we hope that our tenets are orthodox. Upon both subjects, we shall endeavor to preserve that honest neutrality which, whilst it never attacks, is always ready to act upon the defensive."

The posture declared in 1830 was still evident, by implication at least, in some of the last book reviews published in the *Evening Transcript*. The book pages for Saturday, January 11, 1941, contained a review of a new novel, *In This Our Life,* by Ellen Glasgow, a novelist whose great reputation of the 1930s has not survived into the 1970s. The reviewer, Elizabeth Glasgow Howe, liked the book very much, tagging it "the *Vanity Fair* of our day" because of its portrayal of admirable characters who gave indications of direction and meaning to life. She concluded, "Creeds may die, and social orders pass away, but as long as man's fate depends on his own character development, he may with agony and travail work out a world with all things here."

The *Transcript* of February 15, 1941, published a review of Carson McCullers's *Reflections in a Golden Eye* by Margaret Clark. She did not like the novel by an author whose contemporary reputation is certainly greater than that of Ellen Glasgow. In her opinion it was "too preoccupied with the morbid and the bizarre to be the important work every one was expecting from Miss McCullers." She predicted that "it will be talked about in sibilant whispers" because "mental abnormalities interest the young author," who was thereby warned that were she to persist she would produce grotesqueries.

The *Evening Transcript* was not alone in supporting a literary taste that preferred the moral and uplifting to the interesting and entertaining. In *The Proper Bostonians,* published in 1947, Cleveland Amory included a sketch of Mrs. Horatio Lamb, then in her eighties and very much concerned with the youth of the day. She had been collecting books with what she called a "moral uplift" all her life and she was now presenting them to Harvard University to combat what she saw as a trend toward moral decay. She is quoted as saying, "I am a Puritan and a Victorian, and I'll never be anything else until I die. I was brought up on books that held me accountable for every act I did. Their sense of responsibility haunts me, but I believe in them."

Through these same years, books like Erich Maria Remarque's *All Quiet on the Western Front* were kept under lock and key in the "scruple room" of the Boston Athenaeum. At Boston College, there was a section of the library stacks, fenced off in strong chicken wire, commonly referred to as the "cage," where books on the Index of Forbidden Books were kept side by side with books like James Joyce's *Portrait of the Artist as a Young Man*—let alone *Ulysses*—which had in some way offended faculty sensitivities. Nationally the public taste was changing much more rapidly than in Boston. On December 6, 1933, Judge John M. Woolsey, sitting in the court for the southern district of New York had handed down a decision clearing James Joyce's *Ulysses* from the ban which had been imposed upon it by the U.S. Custom's Service. Woolsey had concluded that in the intent of the author he "did not detect the leer of the sensualist," that the presumed effect of the book was "not dirt for dirt's sake," and that its quality must be "judged by average persons."

The decision was upheld against the appeal by the government by the circuit court of appeals with Judge Augustus Hand handing down a decision on August 7, 1934, which took note that "while in a few spots it is coarse, blasphemous and obscene, it does not, in our opinion, tend to promote lust." Then he states what came to be used as a principle in the evaluation of many books which were to be accused of obscenity during the next thirty years, the effect of the book taken as a whole upon the average reader. "The erotic passages were submerged in the book as a whole," the judge noted, "and have little resultant effect." This principle applied to *Strange Fruit* in Boston ten years later would have kept it from being banned, but Boston was going its own way.

The Boston attitude was to be found in the opinion of Judge Manton who, as the single dissenting vote in the circuit court of appeals trial of *Ulysses,* rendered a minority opinion against the book because it was written merely to amuse an audience or enrich the author. "Good work in literature," he opinioned, "has its permanent mark; it is like all good work, noble and lasting. It requires a human aim—to cheer, console, purify, or ennoble the life of people." In Judge Manton's definition of the function of literature one can discern echoes of Victorian attitudes like that of John Ruskin who believed that the only true poetry was the poetry which presented the reader with grounds for experiencing a noble emotion. What differentiated a "noble" from an "ignoble" emotion no court was ever called upon to decide.

By the early 1940s in Boston the arrangement between the booksellers and the police commissioner was beginning to show signs of strain. Early in 1944, for example, Margaret Anderson of the Dartmouth Bookstall was summoned before Judge Elijah Adlow of the municipal court on the complaint of the police commissioner for selling a copy of Erskine Caldwell's *Tragic Ground* which the commissioner had found not to his liking. Judge Adlow ridiculed the charge saying, "It's not for you to try to establish the literary tastes of the community." And he lived up to his reputation for being witty and unpredictable by adding, "The trouble with the police department is they don't have a big enough library." He then concluded by saying he had found *Tragic Ground* dull and that was that.

This was the climate of public opinion about books in Boston when the conviction against Abraham Isenstadt for selling *Strange Fruit,* a book banned as obscene by the police commissioner, was appealed to the supreme judicial court. In 1945, it was the first contemporary work to come before the Court containing the four-letter words which had led to its being called to the attention of the police commissioner in the first place. Curiously enough Judge Qua, in delivering the majority opinion reached by him and Justices Ronan and Wilkins, which found the book obscene, with Justice Lummus dissenting, did not specifically mention obscene language as a factor in their decision. He indicated that the majority, taking into consideration the principle that it was the intention of the work as a whole which must be invoked to determine whether a work was obscene, had concluded that objectionable scenes "occur on an average on every fifth page from beginning to end."

What motivated Judge Qua to condemn *Strange Fruit* seems to have been that a book with so much objectionable material in it might well be "found to lower appreciably the average moral tone of the mass" and, finally, that "the matter which could be found objectionable is not necessary to convey any sincere message the book may contain and is of such character and so pervades the work as to give to the whole a sensual and licentious quality calculated to produce the harm which the statute was intended to prevent."

Strange Fruit was the last book to be banned in Boston and to have its banning completely sustained by judicial review through the various appeal courts and finally by the Supreme Judicial Court for the Commonwealth, taking into consideration not just the obscenity of the language but the intent of the work as a whole.

Three years later the same judges who had ruled against *Strange Fruit*, Justices Qua, Ronan, and Wilkins, joined with Justice Lummus in a unanimous decision of the supreme court which found *Forever Amber* acceptable. Published the same year as *Strange Fruit*, *Forever Amber*, the story of a free-wheeling girl who went from bed to bed during the reign of Charles II, contained none of the four-letter words which had called attention to *Strange Fruit*. A costume romance or, to use a better-established term, a historical novel, it was the first bit of soft pornography published in this country which a woman could read publicly under a hair dryer in the beauty parlor. Its success on the best-seller lists led to a steady parade of imitations which became a staple on the Sunday book pages and paid the rent of many a bookstore for the next decades.

Although the judges agreed that *Forever Amber* portrayed "an unattractive, hedonistic group, whose course of conduct is abhorrent and whose mode of living can be neither emulated nor envied," they seem to have been influenced by the testimony of an expert witness on literature who defended the book as a responsible recreation of court life during the Restoration. He was of the opinion that "it would not be possible to write a historically accurate novel about the Restoration with reference to the court, ignoring the sexual theme." So *Strange Fruit*, which was widely hailed as a significant artistic achievement by reviewers like Edward Weeks in the *Atlantic*, was banned; and *Forever Amber*, which was generally considered to be "without any literary distinction," was exonerated. But the times were changing, and, as long as a book avoided printing the four-letter words that gave judges and community censors some very specific grounds on which to base their adverse decisions, there was, as the 1940s passed into the 1950s, less and less chance of somebody's trying to blow the whistle.

The 1948 decision to pass *Forever Amber* did very little to change publicly confessed canons of taste when compared with the shock waves generated by the publication of another book published that year, the so-called Kinsey report, *Sexual Behavior in the Human Male*, by Albert C. Kinsey. In the years immediately following the end of World War II in 1945, everyone had returned to normalcy believing that "the system" still worked. According to William Manchester, in *The Glory and the Dream* (p. 479), veterans returned from Europe and the Pacific still assuming "that boys who had been properly reared 'saved themselves' for well-bred girls who had remained 'pure'—hence white for brides—and that after marriage and until death they remained faithful to one another." Homosexuals were considered indistinguishable from the criminally insane, and other, wilder forms of aberration were thought to be just the stuff of traveling salesmen jokes.

Then Kinsey's book—275,000 copies sold in 1948 alone—told them the reality was very different from the way in which they had been picturing it: 85 percent of all married men had not "saved themselves" but engaged in sexual activity before marriage; 50 percent of American husbands had committed adultery; 50 percent of American women had not come to the marriage bed "pure." Publication of the companion volume, *Sexual Behavior in the Human Female* in 1953 added further confirmation to Kinsey's original findings that there was such a big difference between private practice and public posture that defense of the tradition: omantic code must be involving many bluenoses in an embarra ng hypocrisy.

No one was neutral about the Kinsey reports. Some were delighted to be able to come out in the open and to be relieved of the secret guilt they had been feeling for what had seemed to them extraordinary behavior. Others, especially those who had been true believers in the Victorian and romantic conception of sex, were horrified. But from 1948 on, it became impossible for a police commissioner or a district attorney to proceed against a book because he thought it offensive to the prevailing morals of the community without checking with Kinsey first.

Through the 1950s, one novel after another slipped by that, in pre-Kinsey years, would have occasioned widespread comment and probably some attempt to ban it. John O'Hara's *Ten North Frederick*, published in 1955, did create a bit of a stir in Boston, not so much because of its explicit references to sexual activity, but because it portrayed all the opinion leaders of a small, traditional eastern community as totally unconcerned with the morality of sexual conduct and only with the problems of achieving some kinds of mutually satisfactory sexual partnerships. In a way they seemed to be acting out one of the conclusions of Kinsey's *Sexual Behavior in the American Female* which maintained "that the reconciliation of the desire for variety and the maintenance of a stable marriage had not been resolved." O'Hara's characters dramatized some successes, some failures, the many difficulties involved in various attempts at resolution. It could be said that public discussion was catching up with actual practice, that art was finally beginning to imitate life after years of having been constrained to imitate only what the establishment was willing to have accepted as life.

The public tolerance for franker and franker portrayals of sex grew steadily during the 1960s and it can be traced through a series of legal decisions involving three notorious novels: *Lady Chatterley's Lover*, cleared in 1959; *Tropic of Cancer*, cleared in 1964; and *Fanny Hill* cleared in 1966. All three decisions were affected by a ruling in the "Roth case" as it came to be called and it has continued to be a landmark case ever since.

Samuel Roth, a poet, publisher and dealer of "not-very-erotic erotica," had been in and out of the courts some five times in the twenty years immediately preceding his conviction in New York in 1955 for sending materials—advertisements, photographs—which had been found offensive through the mails. Roth appealed all the way to the Supreme Court which, when it reviewed the case, linked it with another case, *People of California* v. *Alberts*, which also involved questions of whether or not materials judged obscene were protected by the First Amendment to the Constitution. The progress of this complex case through the courts and the implications of the decision rendered on June 24, 1957, and written by Justice Brennan finding against Roth are clearly summed up in *Literature, Obscenity and Law* by Felice Flanery Lewis (Southern Illinois University Press, 1976, pp. 185 ff.)

In the summary sentence of his opinion, Justice Brennan used what has come to be known as the "prurient interest" formula to define obscenity and concluded that "obscenity is not within the area of constitutionally protected speech or press." From here on for the next several years the definition of obscenity was to be "whether to the average person, applying contemporary community standards, the dominant theme of the material taken as a whole appeals to prurient interest."

There were two other statements in the Roth case which would also be cited in later obscenity trials and which would come to have a great influence in shaping the standards of the community.

One section of the opinion read: "Sex and obscenity are not synonymous. Obscene material is material which deals with sex in a manner appealing to prurient interest. The portrayal of sex, e.g., in art, literature and scientific works, is not itself sufficient reason to deny material the constitutional protection of freedom of speech and press." From now on attempts to ban a book in Boston would have to go beyond calling attention to whatever sexual material, no matter how explicit, it might contain and prove that the material was there to excite prurient interest.

As if to make the demonstration of an appeal to prurient interest even more difficult, the Brennan decision also contained another section which came to have a widespread impact on communities all over America. It proclaimed, "All ideas having even the slightest redeeming social importance—unorthodox ideas, controversial ideas, even ideas hateful to the prevailing climate of opinion—have the full protection of the guaranties (contained in the Bill of Rights) unless excludable because they encroach upon the limited area of more important interests." In succeeding court cases, the prosecution would have to demonstrate not only the appeal to prurient interests, difficult enough to do, but also that the material was utterly without the slightest redeeming social interest, something almost impossible to do, for, when one considers the range of materials which have been preserved in museums because they reflect some aspect of a culture, anything manufactured by a society is of some relevance to an understanding of that society.

The decision that found *Lady Chatterley's Lover* by D.H. Lawrence not obscene was finally rendered by a United States court of appeals on March 25, 1960, which upheld a decision of a lower court. The government decided not to appeal to the Supreme Court and Charles Rembar, the attorney who represented the publisher, Grove Press, himself tells the story of that important trial in *The End of Obscenity* (1970). The book was cleared because of Lawrence's reputation as a writer and because the frank language and erotic scenes were deemed relevant to the portrayal of the relationship that had been central to the author's purpose.

The book became a best-seller. Over six million copies were sold between 1959 and 1960. One can hardly believe that many readers were interested in the book because of its literary value. The judge had been moved to consider it a significant work of art because of the testimony of distinguished literary critics Malcolm Cowley and Alfred Kazin, a critical preface by Archibald MacLeish and a concluding explanatory note by Mark Schorer. But Charles Rembar, who saw it safely through the courts, cannot resist commenting that, with that number of sales, the average person was clearly buying the book, and "the average man, it was pretty clear, was buying because it was a dirty book."

After the clearing of *Lady Chatterley's Lover,* attention shifted to another book which had, for many years, been on the list of proscribed books of the Customs Department, Henry Miller's *Tropic of Cancer.* It also was finally cleared in Massachusetts by a four-to-three decision of the supreme court in 1962.

In the middle of May 1962, *Tropic of Cancer* had its day before the supreme court of Massachusetts. It was the same court which seventeen years before had found *Strange Fruit* obscene and fifteen years before had also found against *An American Tragedy.* A distinguished court consisting of seven judges, five usually sitting on a case, all seven turned out to hear Charles Rembar defend *Tropic.* The attorney general of the Commonwealth, Edward J. McCormack, Jr., presented the case against the book for the state.

The prosecution claimed that the book was so filled with references to filth, sexual and physical, of all kinds, that it could not possibly appeal to anyone without a shameful or morbid interest in such matters. Rembar, who had successfully defended *Lady Chatterley* in the Massachusetts courts, argued that a distinction must be made between the content of a book and the intention of the writer. Some parts of Genesis, he claimed, contained material which might be considered morbid, but that material is certainly not included to appeal to prurient interest. Similarly, though Miller included sordid material in his novel, it was intended for other purposes. Literary critics were cited to show that Miller was considered by some to have been writing a comic novel.

The decision was handed down in the middle of July, four to three, in favor of *Tropic,* reversing the lower court, and thereby becoming the first high court in the country to hold that *Tropic of Cancer* might be lawfully published and enjoy the protection of the First Amendment. Only nine years earlier a federal court of appeals had unanimously declared the book obscene. The majority opinion of the Massachusetts court was written by Justice R. Ammi Cutter and recognized the value of the test of redeeming social significance in determining obscenity.

Judge Cutter concluded that "with respect to material designed for general circulation, only predominantly 'hard-core' pornography, without redeeming social significance, is obscene in the constitutional sense." Continuing as a sitting magistrate, he did, nevertheless, give some indication of what it is not unfair to believe might have been the attitude of a significant part of the Boston community on these matters.

> It is not the function of judges to serve as arbiters of taste or to say that an author must regard vulgarity as unnecessary to his portrayal of particular scenes or characters or to establish particular ideas. Within broad limits each writer, attempting to be a literary artist, is entitled to determine such matters for himself, even if the result is as dull, dreary and offensive as the writer of this opinion finds almost all of the *Tropic.*
> Competent critics assert, and we conclude, that *Tropic* has a serious purpose, even if many will find that purpose obscure. There can be no doubt that a significant segment of the literary world has long regarded the book as of literary importance... We think that the book must be accepted as a conscious effort to create a work of literary art and as having significance, which prevents treating it as hard-core pornography.
>
> [Charles Rembar, *The End of Obscenity,* p. 194]

The attorney general for Massachusetts, then embroiled in a hotly contested campaign for the Senate with Edward Kennedy, did not choose to appeal the decision to the Supreme Court of the United States, and Judge Cutter's decision was widely hailed both within the Commonwealth and across the country as a clarification not only of a difficult legal matter but of a prudent posture for all reflective citizens.

The next case to come before the Massachusetts Supreme Court which had some impact on public attitudes in matters of literary taste involved a book popularly known as *Fanny Hill* but which had already been before the Massachusetts courts, some hundred forty years before under another title. The Massachusetts Reports, volume seventeen, according to Charles Rembar, who was also attorney for the defense in this case and who reports extensively on his problems in *The End of Obscenity* (pp. 314 ff.), record the conviction, following appeal in 1821, of a printer, Mr. Hyde for "publishing a lewd and obscene print, contained in a certain book entitled *Memoirs of a Woman of Pleasure* and also for publishing the same book."

There has always been some confusion over the proper title for this work, originally published in 1748–1749, and over the date of its publication. In a case, similar to that in Massachusetts, the attorney general for the state of Rhode Island stated in 1964, that he "believed the author, one John Cleland, to be deceased." *Fanny Hill* or *Memoirs of a Woman of Pleasure* as published by G. P. Putnam came before Judge Donald B. Macauley in Boston in 1964 and he found it obscene. The prosecuting attorney concluded his presentation with this sincere confession: "I am not a literary expert, although I did major in English in college. I am not one easily offended, but I was offended by this book, and I feel there is no literary merit in it. It did arouse prurient interest and impure thoughts in me."

Putnam, represented by Rembar, decided to appeal through the Massachusetts courts to the Supreme Court of the United States. If *Fanny Hill* were to be found acceptable, it would be difficult to conceive of any book, unless it were what Judge Cutter had called "hard-core" pornography, which could not be found entitled to protection under the First Amendment. Though the ultimate trial of *Fanny Hill* was in the United States Supreme Court, the decision was in response to problems and issues which were raised and defined in Massachusetts courts.

The supreme court of Massachusetts, all seven justices again sitting, heard the appeal from Judge Macaulay's decision against *Fanny Hill* in January 1965 and rendered their decision, reaffirming the decision of the lower court, at the end of March. They concluded, four to three, that *Fanny Hill* had flunked two of the three tests which were now being applied in various ways, either singly or in combination, to determine whether a book was to be considered obscene. Judge Spalding wrote the majority decision and began this way: "Whether the Supreme Court of the United States has laid down three independent standards, all of which ... must be satisfied, need not be decided, for in our opinion *Memoirs* meets all the tests." Another reason why the judges felt they need not be concerned on the issue was that everybody knew the case was headed for the Supreme Court and there they could play the numbers game to determine whether there were one, two, or three tests.

On test number one, whether a book in question appealed to the prurient interests of the reader, Judge Spalding was explicit: "As indicated above, we have little doubt that *Memoirs'* dominant theme appeals to prurient interests and that it is patently offensive." Test number two, whether it was patently offensive, never received any more discussion than the quick affirmation that was contained in that last clause saying it was.

Was the book then "utterly without social importance"? The majority opinion, expressed by Judge Spalding, went on this way:

> We are mindful that there was expert testimony, much of which was strained, to the effect that *Memoirs* is a structural [sic] novel with literary merit; that the book displays a skill in characterization and a gift for comedy; that it plays a part in the history of the development of the English novel; and that it contains a moral, namely, that sex with love is superior to sex in a brothel. But the fact that the testimony may indicate this book has some minimal literary value does not mean it is of any social importance. We do not interpret the "social importance" test as requiring that a book which appeals to prurient interests and is patently offensive must be unqualifiedly worthless before it can be deemed obscene.   [Rembar, 405]

The decision of the United States Supreme Court, rendered on March 2, 1966, reversed the findings of the Massachusetts supreme court, and the majority opinion, written by Justice Brennan, took up just where the Massachusetts decision had left off. In effect Brennan said that a book had to be unqualifiedly without merit in order to be suppressed. If a book had any value whatsoever it could not be deprived of the protection of the First Amendment. He wrote:

> A book cannot be proscribed unless it is found to be *utterly* without redeeming social value. This is so even though the book is found to possess the requisite prurient appeal and to be patently offensive. Each of the three federal constitutional criteria is to be applied independently; the social value of the book can neither be weighed against nor canceled by its prurient appeal or patent offensiveness.   [Rembar, 480]

Thus the state of Massachusetts, and the country as a whole, had come a long way in the twenty years since *Strange Fruit* had been banned because a police commissioner found some words offensive. The tests had become much more complicated; the community had become much more sophisticated in its awareness of the issues involved and much more tolerant of materials which they preferred to let live rather than attempt to suppress at the risk of losing, along with them, some of their own essential freedoms.

For the five years immediately following the Supreme Court clearing of *Fanny Hill,* publishers seem to have enjoyed great freedom in the printing of explicitly sexual material, and the American public made overnight best-sellers of illustrated sex manuals. These were the years of *Everything You Always Wanted to Know about Sex* by Dr. Reuben, and *The Sensuous Woman* by "J." Supreme Court decisions alone could not have accounted for the rapid change in public attitudes. They merely served as milestones marking the steady advance to greater and greater permissiveness in public attitudes.

Couples by John Updike was a best-selling novel in 1968. Graphic in its descriptions of the ways in which six sets of young, married ex-urbanites frequently changed partners in a prolonged sexual squirm that sometimes lasted long enough to be called a marriage, it was tagged a picture of the "post pill paradise." The "pill," of course, was the oral contraceptive, Enovid, which had first been approved as safe by the United States Food and Drug Administration on May 9, 1960. If Kinsey, in his reports on the sexual behavior of the American male and female, was recording the passing of belief in religious sanctions as restraints upon promiscuous sexual indulgence, future commentators would have to record the coming of the pill as removing all social sanctions, such as the fear of unwanted pregnancies, as a bridle on roving sexual expression. Unaware of the social solvent latent in the little pill, the *New York Times* carried the story of the Federal Drug Administration's certification of it as a safe drug on page 75 of its May 10, 1960, issue.

Several other events occurred during the 1960s which eventually led to a public reaction against the new permissiveness resulting in the appointment by President Lyndon B. Johnson of a commission to study obscenity and pornography. As sex had become standard fare in novels, nudity had become expected in many magazines, and by 1966 many movies were of the x-rated variety. What came to be known as the "hippy" culture, with its completely free style of living and use of drugs, reached its peak of notoriety in 1967. The Charles Manson murders of 1969, committed by a hippy-living group on members of the movie industry, finally startled the country into an awareness of what the new license was leading to.

The report of the Johnson Commission on Obscenity and Pornography, delivered in 1970, concluded that "empirical research has found no evidence to date that exposure to explicit sexual materials plays a significant role in the causation of delinquent or criminal behavior among youth or adults." It also stated that "established patterns of sexual behavior were found to be very stable and not altered substantially by exposure to erotica." It recommended that "federal, state and local legislation should not seek to interfere with the rights of adults who wish to do so to read, obtain or view explicitly sexual material." The report was debated in the Senate and was rejected by a vote of sixty to five. President Richard M. Nixon declared it morally bankrupt, and there was a widespread national feeling that much of recently published materials was offensive to many communities.

Proof of a change in direction away from permissiveness was to be found in a series of five precedent-establishing decisions handed down by the Supreme Court on June 21, 1973. Although only one of the decisions dealt directly with a book, all of them had something to do with published materials, and they resulted in establishing a framework of reference which must be considered by any publisher or magistrate trying to determine whether to publish or to censure. Here is the way in which Chief Justice Warren Burger summed up the new tests for determining obscenity:

> The basic guidelines for the trier of fact must be: (a) whether the "average person, applying contemporary community standards" would find that the work, taken as a whole, appeals to the prurient interest ... (b) whether the work depicts or describes, in a patently offensive way, sexual conduct specifically defined by the applicable state law, and (c) whether the work, taken as a whole, lacks serious literary, artistic, political, or scientific value.   [Lewis, *Literature, Obscenity and Law*, 230]

In *Literature, Obscenity and Law,* Felice Flanery Lewis stresses that the most significant aspect of the Burger ruling was the repudiation of the most salient feature in the *Fanny Hill* decision. *Fanny* had been saved on the basis of the criterion developed in the Massachusetts trial, that a literary work had to be completely without social value to be considered obscene. Burger spelled out that this was no longer to work when he wrote: "We do not adopt as a constitutional standard the 'utterly without redeeming social value' test of *Memoirs* vs. Massachusetts." So in a way, in the matter of principle at least, the peak of permissiveness in the publication of overt sexual materials had been defined in the supreme court of the Commonwealth of Massachusetts which had been better known for its banning than its permitting.

For the last three years, as a result of the 1973 decisions, there has been a great deal of confusion nationwide over the limits of the protection provided by the First Amendment to materials which may be questioned as offensive by various communities. The Supreme Court decisions make the reactions of the average person applying contemporary community standards the basic norm for determining whether or not a book appeals to prurient interest. This leaves the question just about where it was thirty-three years ago when *Strange Fruit* came to Boston. It was then found obscene by those applying community standards. Would it be found obscene today? Hardly. Would any book banned in Boston today as a result of an application of community standards have its banning sustained by the Supreme Court? Publishers have been reluctant to probe this terra incognita.

Some indication of the difficulties to be encountered by anyone trying to define community standards was given in an interview with Judge Charles Wyzanski printed in the *Boston Phoenix* for June 29, 1976. The *Boston Phoenix* started out in 1967 as what was then called an "underground newspaper," attacking the establishment, a spokesman for the anti-war movements and student liberal groups. By 1976, it had become a widely read weekly, not an underground publication but alternative journalism. It provided a point of view rather different from that to be found in Boston's established dailies, the *Globe* and the *Herald American,* and was admired for its resourcefulness in undertaking investigations overlooked by the larger papers and respected especially by all the college students in the area for its widespread coverage of movies, recordings, and books. Judge Wyzanski had been a member of the bench of Boston's federal court since 1942 and is known all over the country for his opinions in many landmark cases. The interview is interesting not only for its content but also for its style. It must be recalled that this interview was published in Boston just thirty years after *Strange Fruit* had been banned in Boston for printing some obscenities that had never been in print before and that the ban had been sustained by the Judges Field, Qua, Ronan, and Wilkins.

Judge Wyzanski was asked by the reporter for the *Boston Phoenix,* "What role should the court play, if any, in protecting morals?" He answered at some length:

> Let me begin with the publication of books, magazines, films... So far as I'm concerned, I think the attitude taken by the Supreme Court of the United States during the Warren period is quite defensible. If we are wholly honest, we must realize we are dealing with something that cannot be effectively controlled entirely by the state.
>
> Every male and, I assume, every female from very early life learns by stories, graffiti and the like the intimate details of sexual conduct. No male can go to a public lavatory day in and day out without seeing pictures of genitals in operation and of words. There's nothing new to any male about the term "fuck" or "cock" or "cunt" or anything else. Though this may not have always been true of women... I assume the effect of women's lib and general sexual liberation is that females would find it in women's lavatories. Now everybody knows that public urinals are a chief place of masturbation.
>
> The fact is, most obscene, pornographic things are used for masturbation. They are not used primarily in connection with rapes! They may or may not be used in connection with consensual sexual acts. Nobody who is today a college graduate is unaware of oral sex, is unaware of sexual positions of every kind, anal or otherwise. What are you trying to do? Are you trying to express your own disapproval when you censor such things? Or are you yourself maladjusted in dealing with it?
>
> A judge who is sensible in such matters knows that the state is not today an effective controller. All the state can reasonably do is prevent violence, prevent corruption of the young and also regulate public display.

Obviously the interview could never have appeared in the *Boston Evening Transcript* which had ceased publication in 1941, one year before Judge Wyzanski had been appointed to the federal court.

Recalling the functions of the aedile, a public official in classical Rome responsible for keeping the streets of the forum sweet-

smelling, Judge Wyzanksi went on to point out the problems a modern aedile might have if he undertook to keep our streets free of all offensive materials. Suppose, for example, a "husband and wife, choose nakedly to have sexual intercourse on the (Boston) Common, they have not committed an act of adultery and are not engaging in sin, but they are doing something their neighbors may not all want to watch. A great many of them would like to watch. (He laughs.) But there are people either hypocritically or sincerely who do not choose to watch other people fuck." He then went on to sum up the problems this way:

Now I think there's a lot of hypocrisy. I do not believe you would ever turn away yourself if, unobserved, you could see somebody else fucking, because you have a natural curiosity with respect to this intimate act. Group sex in your age group is more common than in my age group—among other reasons, because people in my age group are not as attractive. Sexual conduct between people who are physically unattractive because of age and other aspects of ugliness is quite a different matter from watching a ballet, let us say, of two people with beautiful bodies, in their teens and early twenties, engaged not merely in simulated sexual intercourse but actual sexual intercourse. I doubt very much if anybody who is totally honest would tell you that he would not like to see a beautiful pair having a sexual act if it was as beautiful as a ballet.

There's a lot of nonsense talked about the subject.

What would Police Commissioner Thomas F. Sullivan, who claimed he had been shocked by two obscenities back in 1944, have done if a copy of the *Boston Phoenix,* reprinting an interview with a federal judge which treated his obscenities as if they were standard informal English, had landed on his desk? The change in community standards which had come over Boston in the years since the end of World War II have been so swift and so great that they are difficult for anyone to grasp.

In *To the Harbor Light* (1976), Henry Beetle Hough, the eighty-year-old editor of the *Vineyard Gazette* famed for his salty editorials, has an interesting observation of this rapid change from a universal reliance upon euphemism to a total explicitness within a generation. He thinks the nation had to undergo a catharsis of hypocrisy. "We would have outgrown the old without the gulf opened by Freud, but we did not need to be shamed (into it), so that we must atone and, as if by way of penitence, adopt the obscene (as I still think of it) as the natural way of speech."

So it seemed for a while during the later 1960s and early 1970s, but the obscenities lost their shock value, and many writers, after paying their dues with a shocker or two, have grown tired of repeatedly proving their right of membership in the club of the liberated by using words everybody knows and that, therefore, add little to everybody's perceptions. Many writers are also fleeing from the leveling effect of the use of the same graphic crudities and seeking more subtle pointings, thereby leaving the past behind.

Also in 1976, Robert Lusty, who had been head of the great British publishing house, Hutchinson, for a generation, published his autobiography, *Bound to Be Read,* and looked back on the years following World War II. "It has been an extraordinary era in which to publish books," he recalled. "Publishing has developed from a comparatively small industry dominated by publishing families into one at least ten times the size, and then only part of an international and interlocking industry of communication almost beyond comprehension."

He then went on, writing specifically of matters of taste:

In the matter of books, when I started with Hutchinson in 1928, their editors would query the use of the word "damn." Strong language, they would suggest in red ink. And now, in recent years, books one would have been expelled for reading in the schools fifty years ago are required reading for juniors. A phrase thought to be taboo in the spring fails to raise an eyebrow in the autumn. I continue to believe that the responsible publisher should retain the ability to be shocked, while ever ready to extend the frontiers of compassion."

That has been the lesson learned by readers, as well as publishers, since *Strange Fruit* making them more responsively and responsibly aware of the human condition.

2

From *The Late George Apley* to *Equus*

The *Boston Post* for October 15, 1944, noted that both Kathleen Winsor and Lillian Smith were visiting Boston to attend publication parties celebrating the launching of their new novels, *Forever Amber* and *Strange Fruit*. On October 22, Miss Winsor gave a lecture at Symphony Hall which was packed, and the *Post* covered her comings and goings as the celebrity she was. That same night, *The Late George Apley* opened at the Colonial, and it was not noticed in the press. It was not until November 12 that the *Post* got around to printing a review by Elliot Norton about the play which, like the novel upon which it was based, presented the country with a character whom many came to think of as the proper Bostonian.

John Marquand's novel *The Late George Apley* had originally been published in 1937 and had gone on to win the Pulitzer Prize. Max Gordon, a successful theatrical producer of those years, saw the possibilities of converting the novel into a play and suggested that novelist Marquand collaborate with George S. Kaufman who had had several Broadway successes. Marquand is reported as having been delighted with the possibilities, quipping, "Great, I know nothing about Broadway; he knows nothing about Boston."

Somehow or other the authors pooled their deficiencies and came up with a play which went into rehearsal in the summer of 1944; tried out in Wilmington, Delaware, in September; spent a week in Baltimore; moved to Boston in late October, and went on to open in New York on November 21. Though it did not win any prizes, it had a long run in New York and toured the country.

In his review of the play in the *Sunday Boston Post* for November 1, Mr. Norton gave it as his opinion that the novel was better than the play which he had found a "little disappointing." He thought that George Apley had been portrayed on stage as "a peculiar and not a typical member of his caste." He also felt that George was, repeatedly, made to look a fool. It is true that George is made, in the play, to seem a fool; in the first act, when he is preoccupied with obtaining credit for being the first to have spotted a yellow-bellied sapsucker; later for his resentment at Cousin Hattie's being buried in the family plot in Mount Auburn Cemetery; then, in the second act, in his discussions with his daughter Eleanor about Cousin Agnes's coming-out party, in his discussions with his wife about Freud, and, finally, about the way in which he is trying to manipulate son John into marrying Cousin Agnes.

The main criticism of the play, however, was that George Apley was not credible because he changed his mind so often. Supposedly brittle and inflexible, he is first portrayed as opposed to son John's affair with Myrtle Dole, the Worcester girl, then he seems to concede the affair might be allowed to develop, then he turns around again and John goes along with him.

But *The Late George,* flawed though it may have been, was great fun in the theater and representative of the gentle satire that Boston audiences could appreciate, even if it were not the generally acceptable portrait of a Boston brahmin the rest of the country took him to be. He was not the kind of fellow who belonged to a very conservative club and whose tastes were reflected in the banning of books in Boston.

For the next decade, from 1945 to 1955, roughly, Boston theatergoers seem to have enjoyed a steady succession of interesting plays like *Magnificent Yankee* (1946), *Mister Roberts* (1948), *Caine Mutiny Court Martial* (1954). During that period Boston was still the great tryout town, and many producers felt obliged to test a new play in Boston before taking it to Broadway. As a result many Boston audiences were the first to see plays which were not quite ready and also plays which never quite made it to Broadway.

Through this period of the late forties and early fifties, along with the obviously Broadway-bound plays, Bostonians were also presented with an opportunity to reflect on more experimental materials. There was *Venus Observed* by Christopher Fry, puzzling in verse style as well as metaphoric content; *Tea and Sympathy* and *Cat on a Hot Tin Roof* with ever increasing explicitness in the treatment of sexual matters. Discussions of Brick's sexual deviations in *Cat,* of Big Daddy's cancer, relied much more on the shock of the moment than the careful pacing of a well-built play, and in these works lay the future.

Some plays Bostonians never got to see because of the author or
the producer's fear of the censor. In 1947 Eugene O'Neill kept *The
Iceman Cometh* out of Boston for fear of having his text mutilated.
Plays had been running into difficulty with the censor just as
books had. Sometimes the problem seemed trivial. When *Life with
Father* by Howard Lindsay and Russell Crouse came to Boston in
1939, the favorite expletive of the main character, Clarence Day,
had to be altered from "Oh, God," to "Oh, gad." Jeeter Lester's
recurring "By God and by Jesus" in *Tobacco Road* had to be sani-
tized into "By gad and by cheese." At other times, the banning was
much more serious in intent and effect. In 1935 Sean O'Casey's
Within the Gates was turned away because some of the local clergy,
Catholic and Methodist, thought it "drenched with sex." It represented a bishop as having fathered, in his seminary days, an ille-
gitimate child and, though he was also portrayed as repentant,
that was enough to keep it out.

It was some time, actually 1960, before the public came to
understand how the city censor wielded such power. In *Broadway
Down East,* Elliot Norton reports on how the Civil Liberties Union
acquired a copy of a letter written by then city censor, Richard J.
Sinnott, to the manager of the Shubert Theater ordering her,
Alice McCarthy, to make several deletions and revisions in a new
play, *Lock Up Your Daughters,* "if it was to continue in the city of
Boston." There was widespread protest that the censor possessed
no such powers. Then in 1963 it was revealed that all producers
and theater managers signed a secret rider to all contracts involving the use of Boston theaters.

In this rider there were eight specific prohibitions outlawing
obscene dialogue, performers mingling with the audience,
females appearing in bare legs, females in leotards, portrayal of
dope fiends, muscle dancing, profanity, portrayal of moral or sexual perversion. The introduction of any material that the censor
could point to as a violation of any of these stipulations broke the
contract and, in effect, thereby denied the production the use of
the theater. Since a lot of money had been invested in productions
before they came to Boston, producers could do little but
comply.

In 1963, when Edward Albee's play *Who's Afraid of Virginia
Woolf?* came to town, Richard J. Sinnott, the Boston censor, wrote
to Saul Kaplan, manager of the Colonial Theater where it was
playing, stating: "It is requested that all use of the Lord's name

wherever it appears in the context of the play be deleted ... It is requested that the expression 'for Christ's sake' also be eliminated wherever it appears." Author, producer, and theater manager felt there was nothing for them to do but comply. The Civil Liberties Union was outraged, and they drew up a carefully reasoned protest to then mayor, John F. Collins. Eventually, there came a reply from the mayor, dated April 8, 1965, which, in effect, ended stage censorship in Boston. A second production of *Who's Afraid of Virginia Woolf?* went on at the Shubert uncensored.

The Civil Liberties Union could hardly have been as successful in securing the cooperation of the mayor had not many changes in public attitudes that had come about since the office of the city censor had been given all its power supported their stand. Books like *Tropic of Cancer* had been cleared of charges of obscenity by the supreme court of the Commonwealth just three years before and the climate of opinion was against further censorship. Still it required courage for Mayor Collins to act as he did for there were still powerful voices in the community, like that of the pastor of the Park Street Congregational Church, who cried out for a retention of city censorship.

What also helped *Who's Afraid of Virginia Woolf?* eventually escape the censor was its timing. The play came along when the American theater was fumbling around looking for new directions to explore. For a decade, it had been without a controversy which might serve as a rallying point for critics and provide them with an opportunity to raise important questions and an audience to test their reactions to some very different fare.

For some eight or ten years before *Who's Afraid* came to Boston, the theater in New York as well as Boston had been searching for a new purpose, a new voice, a new, to use a word which became hackneyed through abuse, "identity." From 1955 on, the line separating the theater from life had become more and more blurred. Life was turned into theater and theater was turned into life. "Happenings," spontaneous, improvised dramatizations were applauded as more honest than rehearsed, contrived plays. Professional plays attempted to include audience participation, either by seating the audience on stage or by having actors move into the audience, and they were thereby forced to provide for some elements of spontaneity, of "happenings." Audiences were startled by the novelty and left wondering how to evaluate these new experiences in the theater which seemed so far removed

from the well-made plays, structured into clear-cut acts, with cur-
tain lines which advanced the plot and a purpose which stood out
clear from the opening scene.
Who's Afraid of Virginia Woolf? was recommended by two distinguished theater critics, John Mason Brown and Edward Gassner
to the trustees of the Pulitzer Prizes for the 1962–1963 award, but
it was turned down and no Pulitzer was awarded for the best play
of that year. The liberal use of socially questionable language can
have been only one part of the problem. The other was the experimental nature of the play which required of audiences that they
think of it in new categories. Eugene O'Neill's *Long Day's Journey
into Night* had been awarded a Pulitzer Prize for 1957, and it, in
many ways, is similar to *Who's Afraid of Virginia Woolf?* As in the
latter play, the Tyrones of the O'Neill play are forever fighting
with each other, jockeying for position, seeking for some recognition in the family. In both plays the major characters inflict pain
upon each other, and in both the drinking provides the opportunity for daring to say those hard truths which at other moments
would have been glossed over.

But *Long Day's Journey* did not challenge audiences as much.
Who's Afraid did in every way. The fights and insults which develop
at the Saturday night party, a party which is a "happening," a
casual outgrowth of a casual invitation, seemed shocking. If such
confrontations occurred in civilized society, it was better to make
believe they never did than to put them on the stage. O'Neill
seemed to be saying that telling too much truth, no matter what
the circumstances, no matter what the provocation, could destroy.
Albee seemed to be saying that the inrush of perception never
could; it helped people find themselves. Violence instead of inhi-
bition might be considered as a means of establishing communication. George and Martha, the older couple in *Who's Afraid,* are
never as close as when they quarrel. On the Saturday night when
they bring another couple, younger, home with them, they drag
them into their fights and soon have them admitting truths about
themselves they never faced before. Here the theater seemed to
be exploring not only new directions but discovering new uses for
itself. Instead of creating illusions, it was pointing to the need to
destroy old illusions. George and Martha have sustained an illusion for years about a child, an illusion which has kept them
going. During the course of the fateful Saturday night they
destroy the illusion they had always said was off limits. They, and

we the theatergoers, will be better off without such deceptions. If honesty is to be preached in the theater, the theater cannot work without complete honesty, and under those conditions, any kind of censorship was destructive of the essence of theater.

In the days of *The Late George Apley* (1945), *Death of a Salesman* (1949), *Caine Mutiny Court Martial* (1954), going to the theater was an occasion for the reaffirmation of common sensibilities. Bostonians who renewed their subscriptions to the Theater Guild shows as automatically as they did their season tickets to the Boston Symphony reconfirmed their sense of community with their shared laughter over Apley's social awkwardness and their shared anguish over Loman's tortured spirit. After 1955 theater audiences seem to have become more and more fragmented. It became more and more difficult for an author to visualize the group which would attend the theater regularly to try to articulate their shared beliefs. So actors and playwrights came to accept the conditions of their art, the absence of consensus in the audience and thus the hollowness of continuing to repeat old myths. The well-made play, which in its structure was an affirmation of belief in the ability to make all experience meaningful, was replaced by the seemingly unstructured play which engaged actors and audience in a mutual search for meaning. First the playwrights, then the audiences, came to accept inexplicitness as inevitable, the staged groping might release, sometimes just through the energy of the acting itself, some residual binding force. Audiences seemed to feel that happening at *Who's Afraid of Virginia Woolf?* Something difficult to define, but certainly very strongly felt, was communicated. Few ventured to attempt a summary of the meaning of the play; many sensed it had shaken them—and stayed with them—more than any of the long-run successes like *Magnificent Yankee* (1940) or *Picnic* (1953).

Beginning with the early 1960s, as many as half the new plays mounted during a season were imports. Robert Bolt's drama about Thomas More, *A Man for All Seasons,* with its hero executed at the end, was certainly not a romantic play but it captured a large audience tired of the trivial and of the sheerly naturalistic. Howard Pinter's *Caretaker* was considered the best play of 1962, but it was not a hit. Audiences found it puzzling, somber, inconclusive. From the beginning, Mick, the hyperactive brother, is portrayed as restless, planning, capable of anything. Aston, the lobotomized brother, is stable, nonviolent. Mac, the third character in the play, is always waiting, waiting to get his identity papers straightened out, waiting to recover his past. What are they all searching for? What is the goal? Pinter gives no clue which might help to pull the play together. Even when compared with a gloomy play like Samuel Beckett's *Waiting for Godot,* Pinter's *Caretaker* seemed heavy and empty. In both plays the characters spoke from vacant stages, their voices echoing through half-empty theaters, readily conveying a sense of humanity's homelessness, facelessness, emptiness. In neither play were the characters even able to formulate the questions they would have liked to ask, let alone come up with some answers. *Godot* did suggest a concept of human nature, but not even that from *The Caretaker.*

Beginning in 1965, there was a growing use of nudity in the theater reflecting changes in public taste and, in turn, affecting what the theater tried to portray. In New York the presentation of full-front nudity can be traced from Robert Anderson's *You Know I Can't Hear You when the Water's Running,* through *Tom Paine,* then *Hair, Massachusetts Trust,* and *Sweet Eros.* None of these was particularly successful except *Hair,* but all were generally considered part of the regular Broadway season from 1960 to 1965. Other productions like *Che!* were even more unrestrained in the use of violent obscenities and extensive nudity, but they were considered to be more experimental off-Broadway productions directed at a different audience. *Oh! Calcutta,* a very successful, financially, series of erotic skits, was much talked about but never treated as serious, legitimate theater. It did, however, contribute to a more general acceptance of nudity in the theater. Critics mentioned the presence of nude scenes less, and audiences began taking them for granted as possible in any play they might attend.

Hair opened in Boston in March 1970, and the censor by that time was less concerned with the nude scene than he was with the irreverent treatment accorded the American flag. Patriotism had become more important than obscenity or eroticism. The attorney general objected to the misuse of the flag in costumes, and that practice in the play was changed.

The next play to open in Boston which went beyond *Hair* in challenging the only restrictions still in effect was Peter Shaffer's *Equus.* "All official censorship in Boston died," as Elliot Norton sums up the history of the problem in his *Broadway Down East,* the night of November 18, 1975, when *Equus* opened at the Wilbur Theater. This play violated almost all of the practices which had been specifically prohibited by the secret rider that had controlled theatrical presentations in Boston theaters until the American Civil Liberties Union finally got Mayor Collins to abolish it. *Equus* included a scene in which a young couple stripped in clear preparation for sexual intercourse. Now there was no restriction upon costuming or nudity left, as there had been no restriction on the use of offensive language since *Who's Afraid of Virginia Woolf?* Boston reviewers now felt the obligation to give their readers some warning of what they might expect as members of an audience of a particular play. Some might not want to be embarrassed by becoming witnesses to total nudity, and many did not want to be embarrassed by having to walk out on what they considered obscene to protect the sensibilities of the members of their families, young or old, whom they had taken to the theater.

For the 1969 edition of Burns and Mantle's *Best Plays,* which was also its 50th anniversary edition, the editor of the introductory essay looked back to 1919 and commented on some of the obvious changes which had come over the theater. In 1921, for example, he noted that there had been 196 plays staged in New York. Not all had been great, admittedly, but they had included Somerset Maugham's *The Circle* and Eugene O'Neill's *Anna Christie.* In 1969, fifty years later, there had been but a dozen new ventures and they seemed to fall into two categories: the experimental and the merely entertaining. Among the latter, *Butterflies Are Free* was the big hit of the year, but many reviewers suspected it. *Butterflies* was a domestic pleasantry which broke no new ground but which diverted its audiences. It provided them with a refuge from the grim existentialist investigations which were their alternate fare. This division of the theater into the light, entertaining, and most likely to be the source of a long-run hit, especially the comedies of Neil Simon, and the experimental, most likely to achieve, at best, but a success of esteem, continues to characterize the situation of the theater today.

Authors can no longer claim, as they did back in the 1940s, that they are being hampered by censorship. In March 1976, *Virginia Woolf* returned to Boston for a revival. Now, to reviewer Elliot Norton, the play seemed so much quieter, and its heroine, Martha, seemed almost tender. In its first venture into Boston, it had been censored. In a second version, it had excited all kinds of controversy. Now its explicit profanity and vulgarity, as well as its techniques, shook up nobody.

In the summer of 1976, Harvard's Loeb Theater brought together in successive performances two plays which symbolized much of what had been happening to theater in Boston over the preceding generation: *Life with Father* and *That Champion Season*. *Life with Father* (1940) had troubled the censor because of the use of "God" as an expletive. Thirty-six years later it seemed remote, like a Victorian period piece, a good illustration of the well-made play reflecting in its every situation a time of comfortable ideals, obvious directions, and many certainties. *That Champion Season* (1971) by Jason Miller had started off-Broadway and been so successful it had moved on to Broadway and success. Four members of a Pennsylvania state championship basketball team gather to celebrate their victories of twenty years before. All in their thirties now, George is mayor of the town and will most likely be defeated in the next election; James a minor school official who runs George's campaigns; Tom, now an alcoholic; and Phil, a successful businessman. There's their coach, the only one who believes in the rightness of a victory they won by cutting corners and playing foul. It's a world as far apart from *Life with Father's* world as possible. Here is a search for values, puzzled individuals all feeling betrayed and reduced to vexation and frustration—an accurate reflection of the world in which the play succeeded.

3

From Amy Lowell
to Anne Sexton

In 1947 Robert Lowell won the Pulitzer Prize for poetry for a collection of his poems entitled *Lord Weary's Castle,* and some critics noted that he was indebted, at least in part, for the incisiveness of his imagery to a relative, a member of an earlier generation and also of a collateral branch of the same family, Amy Lowell. In 1974, he won another Pulitzer Prize for another collection of poems called *The Dolphin.* Between the two books, roughly the same time period we have been studying, the generation which has passed since the end of World War II, his style had changed greatly, the position of poets in the popular estimation had changed greatly, and he, as one of the major influences on that change, had become the subject of numerous studies of his thought and style. In any history of American poetry concerned with the years following World War II, Robert Lowell and Boston will have to figure very prominently for it was here that this weathercock of our literature could be observed by aspiring poet or recording critic.

Robert Lowell set off on his career as poet seeing his calling in terms of old, as a prophet, a seer. In "The Quaker Graveyard in Nantucket," one of his earliest attention-grabbing efforts, he sought to dispense a vision of the injustice of war charged with the defiance of a prophet. The compressed imagery, the careful orchestration of the parts, all building to a grand climax requiring a universal commitment to the avoidance of war hereafter, contributed to a widespread acclaim of the poem as a specimen of what poetry should be. And it added to the interest generated by the poem that it had been written by the descendant of a prominent Yankee family who had broken with the patterns and found a center of belief in Rome.

His later poetry, as in *The Dolphin,* seems much less energetic, more reflective, more like casual conversation. In a *New York Review of Books* essay, Helen Vendler, a colleague at Boston University and close student of Robert Lowell's work summed it up this way: "Poetry, as it is implied in Lowell's late practice, is profoundly irreligious, reality-bound, ordered not by any structural teleology but by a confidence in free association, addressed not homiletically to an audience, but painfully to the self, private rather than public, closer to the epistolary than to the oratorical, as various as conversation in its tonal liberty, free to seem desultory and uncomposed, and, above all, exempt from the tyranny of the well-made."

The publication of Lowell's early poems, his winning of his first Pulitzer Prize, his simultaneous award from the American Academy of Arts and Sciences, had provided Peter Viereck with an opportunity to sing out in the *Atlantic Monthly* for July, 1949: "There has rarely been a year in which more good poets have been published than 1946–47." Among the younger poets he went on to single out, all under thirty-five, all just having published some distinctive poetry, were Richard Wilbur and Howard Nemerov, two poets who would continue to maintain distinctive connections with Boston, but it was Lowell that Viereck thought would stand out as the great poet of the fifties, "for he seems the best qualified to restore to our literature its sense of the tragic and the lofty."

Viereck thought he saw a new love affair developing between the poets and the American public. The two had been alienated for years because so many of the poets had been concentrating on various rhythmic and tonal effects. Now there were signs of a "return to strictness of form and craftsmanship and to lucidity," three qualities which the common reader seemed to respond to. This new formalism in poetry, with its careful diction, Viereck interpreted as a "post-mortem vindication of the literary revolts which began with the Imagists."

The most famous of the imagist poets had been Amy Lowell. Her best-known poem is probably "Patterns" which she wrote in 1915, but it was not included in a published collection of her poetry until *Men, Women and Ghosts* appeared in 1918. It is an expression of rebellion against war by a woman meditating on her lover killed in the First World War in Flanders, and feeling constrained by all the ceremonies, rituals, and conventions which society imposes. The last line of the poem, "Christ, what are patterns for?" was considered too strong for general public taste in 1915, and Amy Lowell was a bit careful in where she submitted the poem for publication. She always included it in her own public readings of her poems for the poem as a whole was very dramatic and the last line most effective. Within months of the poem's publication in the collection of her poems, it was reportedly known by heart by many Wellesley College girls who interpreted it as a protest against all restricting bourgeois conventions.

In "Patterns," for example, in both style and content, Amy Lowell was moving away from writing poetry about those subjects and in a style which had become expected of traditional Boston poets like Oliver W. Holmes. She was pointing in the direction that would be clear in the works of Robert Lowell and other post–World War II poets. But between the two World Wars, the poets who were, for one reason or another vaguely associated with Boston, continued to write about things that did not excite their audiences. It was ceremonial verse as much as anything. In *The Problem of Boston,* Martin Green argues that they were pompous like James Russell Lowell or lightweights like Holmes. Reading through the reviews of newly published collections of poetry appearing in Boston journals in the early 1940s, one is struck by the continuing references to the established authors, people with international reputations like T. S. Eliot, Edwin Arlington Robinson, Robert Frost, W. H. Auden. Their new collections are greeted with appropriate pieties, but, especially in the case of T. S. Eliot, the poems are treated distantly and in general terms. His *Four Quartets,* published in 1943 with the strong Gloucester association of the third poem, "The Dry Salvages," was appropriately praised for its aspirations, but there was no indication of enthusiasm for its intricate rhythms or formidable intellectual explorations. Younger, beginning poets could hardly expect much of a hearing when poetic events of this magnitude created so little attention.

Like a true romantic rebel, Amy Lowell had sensed the need to cut herself off from the immediately past current conventions if they hindered her search for poetic and personal values, and it is this same search which was resumed so much more clearly and energetically by the Boston poets after the Second World War. It was their success that led Peter Viereck to exult so in the 1949 *Atlantic Monthly* article.

There was quite a cluster of poets who began to rise to prominence about that time, and whose connection with Boston was sometimes close, as Richard Wilbur, whose first book of poems, *The Beautiful Changes,* was published in 1947, and sometimes only passing, as John Ciardi. Ciardi taught at Harvard in 1951 and recalls, in *How Does a Poem Mean?* "a number of friends—all of them valued poets—organized a small group that met irregularly to talk about the poems each brought with him. The group continued to meet for two years or so through a number of memorable evenings. The regular core of that group consisted of Richard Eberhart, John Holmes, Archibald MacLeish, Richard Wilbur and myself. I am indebted to those meetings for some of the happiest and best poet's talk I have ever heard." (p. 644).

MacLeish was then teaching at Harvard and won the Pulitzer Prize for 1952 for his *Collected Poems;* John Holmes at Tufts, and, in 1950, Wilbur was appointed an assistant professor at Harvard. In that same year, he published a second collection of poems, *Ceremony,* and won the secure admiration of all critics of poetry. He was repeatedly singled out as writing among the most polished, craftsmanlike verse in America. In the *Paris Review* for Autumn 1953, Eberhart and Wilbur were contrasted. "Wilbur's poems move carefully and elegantly, step by step, calculated to a sure conclusion; Eberhart's are like fireworks left in the rain; many of them have their powder wet, and only fizzle, but when one goes off there is a real explosion."

Richard Wilbur won both the National Book Award for poetry and the Pulitzer Prize for poetry in 1957 for the publication of his *Things of This World.* The reviewer in the *Atlantic Monthly* commented on how Wilbur exhibited "a new-found sense of reality," though the trademark of his work still continued to be a "formal elegance." Both of those qualities come through strikingly in a poem entitled "Love Calls Us to the Things of This World," which begins with the noise of clothesline pulleys awaking an apartment dweller who is then startled by the sight of sheets on the line: "Outside the open window/ The morning air is all awash with angels." The poet's meditation proceeds to a realization of how these washed spirits will eventually have to come down into the world, and ends with a prayer that there be "clean linen for the backs of thieves;/ And the heaviest nuns walk in a pure floating/ Of dark habits, keeping their difficult balance."

Wilbur was then seen as a poet who had gone full circle first losing and then regaining his "lost sense of delight in the actual world." Others were more critical. Donald Hall, in an introduction to *Contemporary American Poetry*, called for Wilbur to break out of the orthodoxy which had ruled American poetry for thirty years. Within that "orthodoxy," he identified two groups: "those who admired the tough density of Donne and those who preferred the wit of Marvell or the delicacy of Herrick." The first group he thought had culminated in Lowell's *Lord Weary's Castle* and the second in Wilbur's *The Beautiful Changes*.

Wilbur went off to Wesleyan as a professor of English in 1959 but never lost his Boston audience. The *Boston Phoenix* always reviews his new books and, though they are not beyond taking a hip-shot at him, they always seem to come out reaffirming the elegance of his craftsmanship. Upon the publication of *The Mind-Reader* in 1976, the reviewer remarked that, "True, there are times when he assumes a quite banal stance, as in 'It is always a matter my darling/ Of life and death.'" And there were times when, to the reviewer, he sounded like bad Ben Jonson, but "as a descriptive, pictorial poet Richard Wilbur is unsurpassed." Maybe Wilbur did not like that judgment, but Amy Lowell would have.

As some of the poets were developing their art in the groves of academe, there were other forces at work in other parts of the country which would ultimately have their effect on the idiom and its preoccupations. Out in San Francisco, Allen Ginsberg, who had worked as an advertising man in New York and Los Angeles before moving there, had a vision as he looked out the window in the Saint Francis Hotel. He entitled the resulting poem *Howl* and it was published by Lawrence Ferlinghetti under the imprint of his City Lights bookstore in 1956. A criticism of America in the cold war with Russia, making the opposition to Russia seem ridiculous, it developed into a very critical examination of all middle-class culture. The poem was first suppressed as obscene, but a judge found some socially redeeming qualities, and by 1960 it was in its seventh printing with more than a hundred thousand copies in print and Ginsberg had won the National Book Award. He was also touring the country, lecturing on poetry, and spreading the gospel of the beats who wanted to drop out of a culture which they found very oppressive. Single-handedly he got a lot of publicity for a group which had been kept out of the literary magazines both in the West and the East and helped define an attitude toward poetry which was at variance with the academic and which made fashionable a protest stance which would characterize the poets of the 1960s. Jane Kramer, in *Allen Ginsberg in America* has him recalling his student days at Columbia in 1945, when John Crowe Ransom and Allen Tate were considered the paradigms of the true poets. He then felt no kinship with them or with Ezra Pound, who was considered a "freak-out," but he did with Walt Whitman for his frankness and, again, with Amy Lowell for her free-style experiments. So the poet as prophet of rebellion, and reexamination hit the road and, like Pied Piper, picked up a following who became excited about the possibilities of saying something revolutionary about the way things were going in the America of the late fifties.

Looking back on those transitional years of the late fifties and early sixties, Adrienne Rich, who won the National Book Award for poetry in 1974, for her *Diving into the Wreck*, recalled "The fifties and early sixties were years of rapid revelations: the sit-ins and marches in the South, the Bay of Pigs, the early anti-war movements, raised large questions. It was then that poets felt they needed time to think for themselves about pacificism and dissent and violence and their place in poetry and society. In the late fifties, I was able to write, for the first time, directly about experiencing myself as a woman." She had broken through the patterns as also had, about that time, Anne Sexton.

Many of Anne Sexton's poems were records of a sensitive woman's encounter with tensions of mid-twentieth-century living. The title of her first collected book of poems, *To Bedlam and Part Way Back,* suggested that the poems be read against the background of her stay in an asylum for psychiatric treatment. Twice she attempted suicide and referred to the attempts in "Wanting to Die" written in 1967:

But suicides have a special language.
Like carpenters they want to know *which tools.*
They never ask *why build.*
Twice I have so simply declared myself.

In an interview with William Heyen, taped at Brockport, New York, on September 11, 1973, she was asked, as she was frequently, to what extent her poetry might be considered "confessional." To what extent had what she wrote about happened to her? She replied: "'Confessional' is a difficult label, because I'll often confess to things that never happened. As I once said to someone, if I did all the things I confessed to, there would be no time to write a poem. So, you know, I mean I'll often assume the first person and it's someone else's story." It was on these grounds that she objected very strongly when someone called her poems "documents for modern psychiatry," but she was never forthcoming about the identification of which poems reflected her experience and which did not.

Along with Anne Sexton and Robert Lowell, there was a third poet, a friend of both and associated in many ways with Boston, who also wrote very personal poetry which has been tagged as confessional, Sylvia Plath. In his introduction to the collection of her poems entitled *Ariel* published in 1965, Robert Lowell, in a roundabout way, admitted that many of the poems reflected the poet's very personal fears and problems. "It is poignant," he wrote, "looking back, to realize that the secret of Sylvia Plath's last irresistible blaze lies somewhere in the checks and courtesies of her early laborious shyness ... Her humility and willingness to accept what was admired seemed at the time to give her an air of maddening docility that hid her unfashionable patience and boldness."

Many of her poems puzzle the common reader with mythological imagery which serves to transmute private experiences that can only be guessed at. In "Ariel," the title poem of the collection, she describes the sense of slight and power she experienced while riding a horse named, after the airy spirit in Shakespeare's *Tempest,* Ariel. She describes her sensations as leading her to identify herself with the flight of "the arrow," and "the dew that flies from off the top of the grass as her horse gallops." Then she becomes "at one with the drive/ Into the red/ Eye, the cauldron of morning," the sun. Again in "Lady Lazarus," she uses an obvious reference to Lazarus who came back from the dead to refer to her previous attempt to commit suicide and to hint at her continuing fascination with suicide. "One year in every ten?/ I manage it. Dying/ Is an art like everything else./ I do it exceptionally well." The last lines proved to be prophetic because she, like Anne Sexton, did succeed in committing suicide after earlier failures.

In a recent book, *Chapters in a Mythology: The Poetry of Sylvia Plath,* Judith Kroll argues against this highly confessional interpretation of Plath's poetry. She claims that "the personal concerns and everyday role [in the poetry] are transmuted into something impersonal, by being absorbed into a timeless mythic system." The attempt to derive a systematic mythic system from haphazard references in the poetry is interesting but not convincing for there is no reason to resort to a more elaborate, hypothetical interpretation when a simple, direct reading of the poems as revelatory of the poet's own experiences will do.

Kroll does not think that Plath's suicide should be "construed as the end of a morbid, tortured, death-loving woman." She does not think that the speaker of the *Ariel* poems "presents herself as sick or neurotic." This, in spite of poems like "Ariel" and "Lady Lazarus" which, as we have seen above, make very explicit references to a recurring death wish. Indeed many of the poems contained in *Ariel,* practically all written between April 1962 and her suicide in February 1963, are sprinkled with imagery which many readers have no difficulty in identifying as suggestive of an infatuation with death. To get out of this difficulty by suggesting a more mythic interpretation of the poems, Kroll has this to say: "Virtually all the apparent 'death-wishes' in her late poems have the ambiguity of a simultaneous wish for rebirth, which can only be achieved through some kind of 'death.' It is not that life itself is unacceptable, 'that life, even when disciplined, is simply not worth it' [as Robert Lowell says in his foreword to *Ariel*], but that life lived on the wrong terms, a life lived by the false self, is not life but an intolerable death-in-life which can be overcome only by dying to that life."

This kind of interpretation will hardly quiet the more direct reactions of many readers who became interested in Anne Sexton and Sylvia Plath because of their tortured responses to the strains of the social tensions of the sixties. Fifteen years after her death, the memory of Sylvia Plath is of a Wellesley girl who attempted and later committed suicide, and of Anne Sexton of a tense neurotic who articulated the feelings and perceptions of many who shared her experiences. Of the Boston "confessional" poets, Robert Lowell, who was their mentor only in part and who wrote, especially earlier in his career on less personal themes, seems to have the only chance of surviving as a major poet.

In October 1967, the year Anne Sexton won the Pulitzer Prize for poetry, Peter Davison, himself author of a recently published collection of poems, *The City and the Island,* wrote an essay for the October *Atlantic Monthly* in which he tried to evaluate who of the poets then writing, some fifty or so, might be considered major. He thought there were then two poets who might qualify: Robert Lowell and James Dickey. Lowell had by then been publishing poetry for more than twenty years and from his first privately printed volume, *Land of Unlikeness* (1944), he had received plenty of recognition. Through that poetry he had, as Davison put it, "looked constantly to the civilized past—to Rome (both pagan Rome and Christian Rome), to the Puritan ethic and the Puritan neurosis, to the city (both in Europe and in America), to the dramatic aspects of poetry, to the sound of voices, to the tradition of Coleridge and Matthew Arnold and T. S. Eliot" for his inspiration (p. 116). Of his poems Davison found "Lord Weary's Castle" (1946) richest in allusions to the American literary tradition, the "Mills of the Kavanaghs" (1951) the most richly melodic and most haunted by New England traditions, and the poems in *Life Studies* of 1959 the most personal. Davison commented, "These poems were shocking in their confessional directness, and they struck their first readers with terrific impact. As one of the book's reviewers, I must confess that my admiration was at first outweighed by my discomfort. Viewed in the perspective of Lowell's total work, *Life Studies* now seems to me his highest achievement."

Were these all the poets who might be considered Boston poets during the last thirty years? Far from it according to some definitions of "Boston poets" which some critics might be tempted to accept. But that is the problem. Some critics would like to define Boston poets to include only those living and writing in Boston, perhaps, even to those influenced by their living and writing here to concentrate on Boston scenes and problems. This would be a very strict definition. Others would seemingly like to include among Boston poets some poets who lived or worked here for a short time while lecturing at any of the local universities.

Then there are problems with the geographical definition of Boston. Some would expand the boundaries of the city to include the metropolitan suburbs like Wellesley, home of Sylvia Plath, and Newton, home of Anne Sexton. Others would spread out to

Amherst and the Connecticut valley to include the poets teaching
and writing at the University of Massachusetts, Smith, Amherst.
That kind of attitude would soon lead to the inclusion of Dartmouth up in New Hampshire and Bennington in Vermont.

Whatever definition of Boston poet is accepted, narrow or
broad, based on geography or subject matter, over the last thirty
years Boston readers have been particularly interested in the
writings of Robert Lowell, Anne Sexton, Sylvia Plath, Richard
Wilbur, Ruth Whitman, George Starbuck, John Holmes—to
name but a few who have clearly been influenced by their associ-
ations with the city and who have, clearly, had an influence on the
taste of the city. That list could be extended very easily—one
readily thinks of James Cunningham, John L'Heureux—for
there are very few poets who have risen to distinction in the last
thirty years who have not been visitors to this city and influenced
by their stay. A major work to be undertaken by one of these poets
must be the impact of Boston and Boston poets on the shaping of
our poetry.

4

From Mrs. Jack to Sylvia Plath

Biographies are the hardy perennials of the best-seller lists. There has not been a year out of the last thirty without a biography or autobiography among the year's most widely read books. In some years, as in 1946, six out of the top ten nonfiction bestsellers were biographies or autobiographies. Two were biographies of President Franklin Delano Roosevelt who had died the year before: *The Roosevelt I Knew* by Frances Perkins who had been his secretary of labor, and *As He Saw It* by his son, Elliott Roosevelt. Two were autobiographical and ranged from the light, bubbling reminiscences of life on a chicken farm, *The Egg and I* by Betty MacDonald, to a grim account of his sufferings under a Communist regime by Victor Kravchenko, *I Chose Freedom*.

In August 1976, *Publishers Weekly,* the trade journal for booksellers, was reporting that biographies were currently among the best-selling categories in stores from coast to coast. Many of the stores had set up special sections for biographies and many booksellers expected them to be among the best money makers during the forthcoming holiday season. They were not disappointed. *Roots*, Alex Haley's account of the pursuit of his ancestors all the way back to their slave origins in an African village, published on September 17, immediately took up residence on the best-seller lists and stayed there for a year. *Hitler* by John Toland also sold very well. But, more interesting as an index to the changes which had come over the writing of autobiography during the last thirty years, were two other bestsellers: *My Parents* by James Roosevelt and *Bubbles* by Beverly Sills. James was indiscreet in discussing his father's relationship with various women and unreserved in talking about the relations between his mother and father, matters which Elliott would never have dreamed of mentioning in his biography thirty years earlier. Beverly Sills, reminiscing about the rocky road she traveled on the way to the top of the opera world, was completely frank, uninhibited in a way that Betty MacDonald, writing of life on a farm, never even hinted at.

In his monthly column, "The Peripatetic Reviewer," for the *Atlantic* of December 1943, Edward Weeks took up the question of where biographer or autobiographer ought to draw the line between "matters of legitimate private interest and those of legitimate public interest." He sensed a momentum growing which would impel autobiographers to be more and more confiding lest they not be considered sincere. "An autobiographer without reticence," he wrote, "is usually an author without self-respect."

This problem of what to tell and what not to tell is an old one. Upon the publication of Boswell's biography of Samuel Johnson, Mrs. Montagu, a friend of Johnson's, was indignant and is quoted as asking, "Would any man who wished his friend to have the respect of posterity exhibit all his little caprices, his unhappy infirmities, his singularities?" Boswell obviously believed that Johnson was a strong enough figure to bear a few blemishes. Perhaps Lord Moran, private physician to England's World War II Prime Minister, Winston Churchill, felt the same way for in a biography, *Winston Churchill: The Struggle for Survival,* he revealed details about Churchill's health, his personal habits, bits of conversations he had overheard in the course of his professional duties. In a letter to the *Spectator,* published in the issue of May 26, 1966, Lord Chandos severely criticized the biography because it revealed details and confidences of the sickroom, "secrets of which— obtained by a physician—should be almost as closely guarded as those of the confessional." The *Times,* in an editorial, took up this theme and tagged the book as "a grave violation of the ethical code," and the British Medical Association went on to censure Lord Moran.

Most people would assume that there are limits to what may be revealed and by whom. Sometimes these limits can be established by reference to professional codes of conduct as in the case of Lord Moran where the professional ethics of the medical profession should have controlled the content of his biography. Most of the time, however, there is no ready code to which a problem of discretion can be referred. It becomes a problem of taste and prudence for the biographer as it was for Samuel Johnson, who, in his

Rambler #60 essay back in 1750 wondered whether Joseph Addison's heavy drinking should ever have been made public.

Some sense of the dimensions of the problem can be gained by contrasting two treatments of the suicide of Harry Crosby, one by Edward Weeks in *My Green Age* published in 1975 and the other in *Black Sun* by Geoffrey Wolff published in 1976. Weeks knew Harry Crosby and his wife, Caresse, as very close friends both here in Boston and abroad in Paris where they lived most of the time. This is how he recalled time they spent together in the summer of 1927:

> We saw a good deal of each other in that summer of his return, sometimes at parties and more casually after Caresse had taken the children to visit her mother at Nantucket. Harry was lonely in his old haunts. Fritzy and I had rented a little cottage in Ipswich and from there he and I roamed Coffin's Beach or the Essex Woods, talking of writing and the future while I tried to separate the man from the legend he was beginning to create. He was reputed to be a great lover, yet his devotion to Caresse seemed unshaken and he always came back to her. His philandering did not square with my idea of fidelity but if she ignored his swordsmanship, why shouldn't we? Paris had cultivated his taste for wine and he was a steady drinker; he was still gambling—and losing—heavily at the races, and, of course, there was talk of drugs. These extravagances concealed from old friends how serious was his intent to be a writer and how often he struggled against his dissipations.

There we have the objective and sensitive biographer; objective because he does not conceal facts or rumors; sensitive because he does not exploit them to create a sensation at the expense of his overall purpose which is to recall an interesting and colorful personality. A little later, with the same sense of taste and proportion, Weeks tells the story of Harry Crosby's suicide.

> On December 10 [1929] in Stanley Mortimer's apartment in New York, in a suicide pact, Harry shot his enchantress, Josephine, and then himself. Archibald MacLeish went quickly to the scene and was present when the medical examiner finished his examination.

"I pity that poor devil," said the doctor.

"Yes?" said MacLeish.

"Yes. After shooting her he sat here for five hours before he turned the gun on himself."

At that time all I was aware of was pity. Why? Why? I thought as I went over to 95 Beacon Street to see his parents.

The note Weeks is continually trying to strike in his recollections of Harry Crosby is summed up, approximately, in that "Why?" Why did Crosby do it? What is the explanation for the tragic end of all that unfulfilled promise? It is the question frequently posed in tragic studies without any expectation of a clear answer and we do not get one here either.

On the other hand, here is the way in which Geoffrey Wolff tells the story of the Crosby suicide in *Black Sun*. The sequence in the presentation of the details must be noted, for it, as much as the details he chooses to incorporate, contributes to an emphasis on the scandalous and the morbid. Wolff is not trying to comment, "What a tragedy was here!" but "What a gruesome, selfish ending!"

The headlines the next morning added up the lurid sum: TRAGEDY and DISGRACE. Decades later, a distant cousin of Harry's, Clark Grew, read something at Harvard about his notorious kinsman, and from curiosity asked his grandmother about the poet, till then unknown to him: "She just froze when I mentioned his name. She was in New York with my grandfather to go to the theater, and she came out of the theater at eleven o'clock, and there was some guy selling the local rag: *"Extra! Extra! Poet found dead in apartment with Boston girl!"* My grandfather turned to my grandmother and said: "We will never mention his name again." And they didn't.

The biographer, by presenting the reaction of family members to the suicide first, is defining the reaction he expects of his readers, which he hopes will be one of shock similar to that experienced by the relatives. In the paragraph which follows, he is trying to recreate the event in a way which will support his tagging it as "lurid."

They were discovered lying together in the bedroom upstairs off the balcony, beneath a silk coverlet and dressed except for their bare feet. Mortimer (Crosby's friend who had let Harry have the use of his apartment for the lovers to meet) had reached the studio shortly after 9:30 and tried the door: it was bolted from the inside, and no one answered his knock. He called for the building's superintendent, who broke in with a fire ax. Harry was gripping in his right hand, as though for dear life, a .25 caliber Belgian automatic. There was a bullet hole in his right temple, and a bullet hole in her left temple. His free arm was wrapped languidly around her neck, and their left hands were clasped. They faced each other. She was still wearing her orchid.

This kind of writing is seemingly less interested in seeking answers than in revelling in details. And yet, how reliable are those details? How does the biographer know that Harry was clasping the gun "as though for dear life," and that his arm was "wrapped languidly" around Josephine's neck?

If the justification for a biography which dwells on details like this is that it is an attempt to present the whole truth, then it is worth reflecting on its reliability by contrasting this account from *Black Sun* with Archibald MacLeish's exchange with the medical examiner, Dr. Norris, and the account as given by Edward Weeks just quoted above.

Caresse [Crosby's wife] would not go to the studio to witness the carnage. Instead she telephoned Archibald MacLeish, who was in town from his Massachusetts farm to see his friends from Paris. She begged MacLeish to take charge; when he was admitted as Mrs. Crosby's ambassador to the ninth floor of the Hotel des Artistes, the first man he noticed was Dr. Charles Norris, the medical examiner. He was pacing up and down like a tragic figure in a Sherlock Holmes story. "That's quite a friend you've got there." He was fascinated by Harry's looks, thought he was wonderful-looking. Norris told MacLeish that Harry had let himself live at least two hours longer than Josephine.

Readers will readily notice the very obvious factual difference between the Wolff and the Weeks accounts: in Weeks's Crosby is reported to have let himself live five, in the Wolff story only two, hours after shooting Josephine. But that substantive difference is relatively trivial in its contribution to the difference in final effect which is more the result of sequence and emphasis.

In 1976 a flood of exposés of the private misconduct of some congressmen like Wayne Hays of Ohio led publications like *Time* to editorialize that it seemed as if we were in some danger of becoming a nation of voyeurs. In its June 14, 1976, issue, it took this stand: "Editors might hesitate to describe as voyeurism the public tastes they cater to, but they do constantly broaden their standards of what is fit to print. The direction is mostly downhill, or toward more freedom, depending on your point of view. After all, women—Congressmen's girl friends, President's bedmates— now gleefully sign book contracts to describe conduct that once would have earned them a scarlet A as a branded adulteress."

The direction had indeed been downhill for some time. Way back in 1890, Louis Brandeis, then a young lawyer, wrote that "the press is overstepping in every direction the obvious bounds of propriety and of decency. Gossip is no longer the resource of the idle and of the vicious, but has become a trade, which is pursued with industry as well as effrontery." What his comments would have been had he been able to read *Black Sun* or some of the confessions of congressional and presidential ex–girl friends can only be left to wonder. Times change, and change rapidly. Writing in the 1890s, Brandeis expressed himself as if there were no room left for more salacious gossip. What looks to us today like the ultimate in public confessing may, a decade hence, also have come to seem comparatively restrained.

Historians of the biographical form, like Professor James L. Clifford in *From Puzzles to Portraits,* recognize different kinds of biographies, each governed by a different overall purpose and each, therefore, with a different attitude toward total revelation. They range all the way from the biography, frequently multi-volumed, which attempts to present a total record of the subject's life, keeping interpretation to a minimum, to a biographical novel which admits private speculation to fill any gaps in the record. In between are the complete interpretive study, which attempts to provide an overall understanding of the subject–character and of as much of the record as possible, and the portrait, which frankly admits to being a limited study but which also tries to be as faithful as possible to all the relevant documents.

Illustrations of the kind of biography which has set itself the goal of maximum preservation of the record and minimum interpretation of its significance are subject to question. It may be argued that the process of selection and placement of documents in a sequence constitutes an interpretation, just as the decision by a newspaper editor to "play" a story on page 1 or page 10 constitutes editorial interpretation. Two biographies, one complete, one in process, may serve as illustrations because their authors have professed that they intended to assemble the record which others might interpret. Edward Nehls opened his three-volume biography, *D. H. Lawrence*, with the statement: "In assembling this composite biography of D. H. Lawrence, I have been guided by the single desire to collect and preserve as much trustworthy material as I could locate, and to give each contribution its full significance by proper placement in a context." To that intention, Professor Nehls remained consistent throughout his work.

In similar fashion historian Martin Blumenson is collecting and arranging in *The Patton Papers* the documents related to the life and World War II campaigns of the famous general. The inclusion of documented scandal in a biography of this kind can certainly never be considered amiss. Lord Moran, Churchill's biographer who was censured by the British Medical Association for including material he had come by as Churchill's private physician, defended himself by admitting the obligation to respect privileged conversations during a person's life, but he then went on to argue that this obligation ceased, if it was not indeed reversed, after the death of a famous person about whom the public had the right to know the whole truth. Anyone learning of scandalous material through a professional relationship was bound not to reveal it as long as the patient or client lived, and the courts should protect him from any constraints which might be applied to try to make him break his trust. After a public figure's death, posterity's right to know all that might help in the understanding of past or present might be considered to take precedence over an individual's right to privacy. Looked at this way, the individual's right to privacy ceases with his death, and biographers are then free to review and reveal the entire record.

Multivolume biographies are more likely to be the researcher's tool than the common reader's frequent fare. They rarely make the best-seller lists and must be sought out in the larger libraries. The general reader is more likely to pick up a biography from the opposite end of the spectrum, a fictionalized re-creation of a person's life composed of varying parts of fact and imagination. They were a staple of the book trade in the fifties and sixties but have since faded in popularity. One of the most successful was Irving Stone's long, novelized interpretation of the life of Michelangelo entitled *The Agony and the Ecstasy*. It topped the best-seller lists of 1961 and was later made into a movie well remembered for its spectacular scenes and spectacular profits. The author then went on to similar treatments of the lives of John and Abigail Adams in *Those Who Love* (1965) and of Henry and Sophia Schlieman, the amateur archaeologists who located the site of ancient Troy, in *The Greek Treasure* (1975). These last two, like their many imitators, were not as successful, though they were all carpentered according to the same blueprint: a heavy display of facts to authenticate the backgrounds and outline the main dates of their subjects' lives, but an even larger amount of pure speculation in the form of unrecorded incidents to make the plot move more rapidly and to make the relationships among the main characters more dramatic.

Whenever the value of such fictionalized biographies is questioned, defenders of the genre frequently cite Robert Graves's *I, Claudius* as an example of how the form, if it can be dignified with that term, can be used to illuminate a stretch of history. Graves, a classical scholar, using the Roman historian Tacitus and other writers of Imperial Rome for his sources and point of departure, created a fictitious autobiography supposedly written by the famed Roman emperor Claudius filling in the six years preceding his coming into prominence in A.D. 47 for which there is no record and which were undoubtedly among the most important in the shaping of his policies. More recently translated into a television series which has been shown several times over public television stations, *I, Claudius* has achieved an authority and authenticity which its original author certainly did not anticipate. It is a brilliant speculative attempt to fill in the historical record and, as such, deserves a hearing. There have been any number of similar attempts to fill in the seven lost years in Shakespeare's life, from the time of his leaving his hometown of Stratford-on-Avon in 1585 until he is reported in London in 1592, all interesting to anyone wondering where and how Shakespeare learned to write plays. But none of these attempted reconstructions should ever be confused with historical fact. If biography is a form of history, and if the purpose of history is to reconstruct the past as accurately as possible, to tell it as it truly was, then these fictionalized biographies are not to be confused, as they sometimes can be in the popular estimation as the result of an intense publicity campaign, with true history.

Historians prefer the novelized biography which is readily recognizable for what it is, like Irving Stone's treatments of Michelangelo and the Adamses, to those biographies which, more carefully controlled, sometimes read like scholarly productions. Through the late 1950s in France, Maurice Druon wrote a series of studies on the last of the Capetian kings which won high acclaim from historian as well as the general reader. *The Iron King,* published in this country in 1956, on Philip IV of France was probably the best of the series and it had many readers believing that what they were learning about the early fourteenth century was gospel.

More recently in this country Cecelia Holland has done a series of historicals, some mainly biographical, like her first, *The Firedrake* (1966), an evocation of William the Conqueror, which are fair representations of the form where intriguing fact, certified by the existing record, shares the page with numerous suppositions and even wild imaginings without any warning to the reader of which is which. Recognized for what they are, these biographies, or supposed autobiographies, can never raise any questions about the admissibility of propriety of their use of gossip, scandal, or shocking anecdote. Those are their stock-in-trade and the buyer reading to be entertained or diverted should not delude himself into believing he is doing anything else.

Far removed from the novel-biography but close to the exhaustive compilation of the surviving record in its scrupulous adherence to the documented is the scholarly interpretive biography. These are the biographies that, at one and the same time, hope to be definitive in their presentation of their subject, but also to interest a wide public in an appreciation of their subjects' achievements. Biographers in this group try to include as much of the record as possible and they are frequently criticized for trying to do too much. Mark Schorer's *Sinclair Lewis* (1961) was criticized by one reviewer as being "utterly befeathered in facts." Another thought Schorer had been guilty of the "exhaustive fallacy in biography," suggesting: "Had he spared us the tedium of so much of Lewis' daily life, had he cut his book by half, he might have shown us Lewis as he really was."

This same criticism was leveled at Michael Holroyd's detailed study of the critic Giles Lytton Strachey, *Strachey* (1967). Holroyd was thought "boring because he reproduces every inconsequential letter in full, though one Strachey letter is very much like another." John Unterecker's life of the poet Hart Crane, *Voyager* (1969), also was criticized because the author was "unable to present what was typical and to let the rest go."

All of these biographies published during the last decades were widely read, recognized as near-definitive in their summaries, but still rebuked for being too inclusive. Treading the narrow path that separates the too-much, on one side, from the too-little, on the other, is just another of the many feats expected of the successful biographer. The experienced tend to lean toward the side of including a bit too much. They know that it is sometimes necessary to convey a sense of authority by the presentation of a great density of detail. Some of these critics of the biographer who has indulged in what they seem to consider "overkill" by including too much seem to echo the fool in *King Lear,* who counsels,

> Have More than thou showest,
> Speak Less than thou knowest.

There are certainly times when the fool's counsel is wisdom, but there are others when a full disclosure of the record is needed for the biographer to be convincing. He builds his authority by showing how extensively he can support his position.

In *Biography: The Craft and the Calling* (1969), Catherine Drinker Bowen, herself a very successful biographer of the Adams family and Sir Edward Coke, the early seventeenth-century jurist, tries to help the academic historian whose main object may have been to recover and publish something hitherto unknown about his subject to attempt the more difficult interpretive biography which depends upon his ability to shape for a large audience a consistent view of his subject. It is not enough, she insists, for a biographer to assume that all he has to do is to tell a coherent story and everyone will delight in it. On the contrary, he must have a consistent view of the subject, and that view must exercise a control on all that is included and provide the basis for excluding a lot of material.

In a sense she is saying what James Clifford also pointed out in his *From Puzzles to Portraits,* namely, that the best biographers are creative artists who have a view of their subject, and that view is what helps them decide which anecdote to include and which to omit. The decision as to the relevance of an anecdote must be reached in terms of a preconceived picture, and the biographer must sustain that view throughout his entire work if the book is not to be but a collection of note cards of undigested material.

One illustration of the way in which a biographer's vision succeeded in imposing a dominant interpretation of his subject is John Mack's Pulitzer Prize–winning biography of Lawrence of Arabia, *Prince of Our Disorder* (1976). Here the documents are just slightly less numerous than the problems. The main problem is to explain Lawrence's strange reclusiveness throughout his life and his turning to flagellation and masochism in his later years. As Mack sees it, the explanation is to be found in the way in which he was dominated from his early days by a sense of guilt: his mother and father were not properly married; she was always urging him on to achievements he couldn't quite reach, and then, while serving with the Arabs, he was caught by the Turks and subjected to sexual assault wherein he did not behave as he felt he should have. The biographer sees in these experiences the events that controlled all his feelings of inadequacy, and that explain his near-heroic endurance, the taking of Aqaba, and his sense of inferiority in later life. Mack's biography provides a better basis for understanding why T. E. Lawrence felt so guilty and so determined to achieve in order to compensate, and, thus, a better basis for understanding the surviving documents than any other.

Another recent biography that attempts to grapple with a similarly difficult personality to come to understand, but which does not succeed as well, is *Evelyn Waugh* by Christopher Sykes (1974). Sykes was a close friend of the prickly novelist and in his biography tries to make out the best possible case for Evelyn who was consistently critical of his fellow man both in life and in the satirical portraits of his novels. Waugh envied everyone and yet tried to give the impression that he himself was completely detached from the affectations that made others seem foolish. Sykes was criticized by reviewers for his revelations of Waugh's sexual preferences and drinking habits, and his revelations that Waugh was literally ready to go down on his knees to beg a knighthood or similar recognition in the annual award of honors by the king. What seems to be lacking in Sykes's biography that is present in Mack's is a consistent interpretation of the subject's life. Mack traced through Lawrence's life a recurring preoccupation with guilt and compensating desire to achieve; Sykes follows Waugh's life through a series of stages without suggesting any theme. As in many good but not great biographies, Sykes has not come up with a convincing definition of some integrating principle which might have illuminated the life and organized the biography.

The last kind of biography to be discussed here according to the classification we have been developing is sometimes known as the "portrait." It is frankly limited to a picturing of some section or aspect of a subject's life. Gamaliel Bradford, a Massachusetts author who died in 1932, had a name for this kind of biographical word painting as he practiced it, the "psychograph." *Lee, the American,* published in 1912, was the first book wherein he followed his technique and which caught on with the American public.

Herein he sought to isolate the characteristic strand in a person's life and point to its effect in all the affairs of his life. His most successful venture in this form was *Damaged Souls* (1923), which described what he thought were the underlying characteristic traits reflected in the lives of such Americans as Aaron Burr, P. T. Barnum, and Thomas Paine. Edward Wagenknecht, for many years a professor of English at Boston University, continued to write psychographs in the tradition of Gamaliel Bradford and is well remembered for his studies of T. R. Roosevelt and Longfellow.

The true immediate ancestor of the psychograph was most likely Lytton Strachey in his *Eminent Victorians* (1918) wherein he sought by a few quick strokes to "hit off" the character traits of Cardinal Manning, Florence Nightingale, and General Gordon. Strachey was widely criticized for his freedom in the treatment of the record and answered that "uninterpreted truth is as useless as buried gold." Studying portraits like these, the reader has to bear in mind that the lighting of the picture is being artfully controlled.

In 1956 then Senator John F. Kennedy wrote a best-seller, *Profiles in Courage,* which could be viewed as a gallery of portraits of American politicians who had distinguished themselves for political courage in the face of voter opposition. The men were not the best known in our history but included Lucius Lamar, a Reconstruction congressman from Mississippi, and were from both sides of the political fence, Republican and Democrat. All had one common note, independence and integrity under pressure.

Of John Quincy Adams, the late President Kennedy wrote:

When Jefferson on September 18, 1807, called upon Congress to retaliate against the British by enacting an embargo effectively shutting off all further international trade—a measure apparently ruinous to Massachusetts, the leading commercial state in the nation—it was John Quincy Adams of Massachusetts who rose on the Senate floor and called for referral of the message to a select committee; who was appointed Chairman of the committee; and who reported both the Embargo Bill and a bill of his own preventing vessels from entering American waters.

"This measure will cost you and me our seats," young Adams remarked to a colleague, as the select committee completed its work and its members made their way to the Senate floor, "but private interest must not be put in opposition to public good."

Adams was prophetic, for the local papers called him a "popularity seeker," a "party scavenger," but Adams had the courage to stick by his position. Seeing Adams from this point of view is seeing only part of a complex man involved in many more affairs. But isolating a trait in order to bring out that aspect of the character is no more unfair than for a portrait photographer to so arrange the lighting that some feature of his subject—forehead, eyes, chin—is highlighted in order to suggest some predominating characteristic.

In the mid-forties, the attitude of most Bostonians writing biographies or themselves subjects of biographies would have been one in favor of restraint and discretion. In 1976 Lowell Thomas published the first volume in his autobiography, entitled *Good Evening, Everybody* from the tag line he had used to sign off his daily news broadcast for forty years. In his book Thomas states explicitly that he did not consider himself "an oracle"; that age had given him just "enough wisdom to reserve exposure of my inner soul to God and my wife." That was, fortunately, the attitude of most biographers, and it was reflected in biographies like that of Louise Hall Tharp of Isabella Stewart Gardner known as *Mrs. Jack* (1960).

Mrs. Gardner had been the subject of many an anecdote throughout her life. She had even been the subject of a very satiric poem by Boston brahmin poet John Wheelwright entitled "Man?"

and written in the 1920s. Wheelwright used a number of anecdotes about Mrs. Gardner to raise questions about the nobility of this creature man as Irving Babbitt, then at the height of his fame as a Harvard teacher, saw him. Part of the poem went this way:

> When young (because her things-in-law were Gardners)
> She was invited to my Grandmother's Party.
> Her footmen bore her light, white-satin litter
> straight up the flying stair Bulfinch designed,
> and set her down (thump-thump)—in the Back Parlor.
> Thus did she lie on lilies and roses
> in a white satin cuirass she could not stand in
> with Parma violets at either hip bone
> while Men crossed and uncrossed their legs all evening,
> like bees who cluster around a honey cluster.
> All this, because She said, she sprained her ankle.
> The levee ended when her footmen entered
> and my grandmother said: "Recumbent Lady,
> I hope that when you come again you will be
> perpendicular, not horizontal."

In her biography of Mrs. Gardner, Mrs. Tharp had to evaluate any number of legends like these which had grown up around the memory of her subject. She did it with detachment, attempting, in all cases, to identify the origin of the story and to give some indication of why some had persisted.

The beginning of the proliferation of stories about Mrs. Gardner seems to have been upon her return from a trip to Europe in 1868. She had left in the late spring, a rather typical Victorian lady suffering from a very fashionable disease then called "neurasthenia," and had actually been carried on board ship in a litter. When she returned in October, she became the talk of the town. While abroad something had happened to give her, as we might say today, a new image of herself. She had bought an entire new wardrobe at Worth's in Paris, and, instead of putting the clothes away for a year as was customary with some Boston matrons who thought it gauche to be seen in something obviously new, Mrs. Gardner wore hers right away. She had abandoned the old hoop skirts and lifted her hem lines. So one of the first stories to start the rounds that fall was of a friend—sometimes identified as male, sometimes as female—who supposedly inquired of Mrs.

Jack, "Pray who undressed you?" To which she was reported as replying: "Didn't he do it well?"

Among the stories of Mrs. Jack that Mrs. Tharp treats with restraint is one, as it is included in Wheelwright's poem, in which "She scrubbed down the altar steps every Good Friday." In lengthier versions, she is reported to have scrubbed down the stairs of the Church of the Advent in the Back Bay on Good Friday in expiation of some great, secret sin. Mrs. Tharp could not trace the origin of this story nor could she guess what secret failing might be hinted at.

In a Boston where so much of behavior was prescribed by conventions, written or unwritten, the least divergence could attract notice. Reading through the *Boston Evening Transcript,* no one can help noticing how thoroughly social gatherings of the people who counted were covered. At important funerals more than one reporter was assigned, so they competed with each other to find something to write about that would be different. Mrs. Gardner rarely disappointed the gentlemen from the *Transcript* who covered her soirees. She did not let them down at her funeral. In her will, she stipulated that her coffin was to be carried on the shoulders of her pallbearers. And so it was done.

If Louise Hall Tharp's biographies of Isabella Stewart Gardner, the Peabody sisters, and Sam Ward can be used as illustrations representative of the kind of interpretive biography which was fashionable during the fifties and early sixties—always remembering that writing on such important Boston subjects she was subject to very close scrutiny by Boston reviewers—then Stephen Birmingham's *The Late John Marquand* (1972) might serve as an illustration of the kind of biographical writing which came into fashion in the later sixties. When Boswell's biography of Sam Johnson appeared, Hannah More, a friend of Sam's, was quoted as saying, "This new fashioned biography seems to value itself upon perpetuating everything that is injurious and detracting." So at times it seems with many of the most recent biographies. In Birmingham's study of John Marquand, we are not disappointed. The title, *The Late John Marquand,* obviously invites some kind of comparison or contrast with Marquand's first very successful, and perhaps best-remembered, work, *The Late George Apley.* The two works were published some thirty years apart, like so many other works we have been contrasting, and come from completely different worlds. Aspects of the late George's life the late John would never have considered introducing into a biography, the current Stephen revels in: Marquand's poor relations with his wife and his prolonged relations with Carol Brandt, wife of his literary agent and friend.

In his biography, Stephen Birmingham repeats an anecdote that may be revealing of his subject, John Marquand, but it is not without its obvious applicability to Birmingham's own writing.

> Some months later, (after recovering from a heart attack) when he was able to get down to New York, novelist Louis Auchincloss recalls meeting Marquand at a party at the Thomas K. Finletters'. John was back in his old form, swinging his glass in his hand as he entertained his audience, holding forth on what he called "the lack of taste and reticence" in younger American writers. A few minutes later, as he was talking about his weeks in the Newburyport hospital and how, as part of his therapy, an abdominal massage had been prescribed. His nurse, John confided, had whispered to him during the procedure, "How lucky I am to be able to manipulate the lower abdominal muscles of a man like you." One of the guests at the gathering was the New York *grande dame* Mrs. August Belmont. When Marquand had finished his anecdote, Mrs. Belmont inquired, "And where, Mr. Marquand, was the taste and reticence in that remark?"

Marquand's attitude seems to have been that discretion is something for others to observe. As far as I am concerned, a good story is a good story. Stephen Birmingham seems to share that attitude. Mrs. Belmont's attitude was that of an earlier generation, a generation to which Marquand liked to make people believe he belonged and from whose point of view he had been criticizing the behavior of a more recent generation. The conflicts—not to mention possible hypocrisies—are obvious.

More recent writers have become even less reticent as can be readily illustrated from a new biography of Sylvia Plath by Edward Butscher, *Sylvia Plath: Method and Madness* (1976). On August 15, 1953, Sylvia, home from her sophomore year at Smith College, tried to commit suicide at her mother's home in Wellesley by taking an excess of sleeping pills. This attempt became the central incident in her autobiographical novel, *The Bell Jar,* which was first published in England in 1963 and in the United States in 1971. After graduating from Smith in 1955, she went on to Cambridge where she met the British poet Ted Hughes whom she later married. In 1959 she returned to this country to teach and attended lectures on poetry given by Robert Lowell at Boston University. She was part of a small group including Anne Sexton and John Starbuck who frequently adjourned after the conclusion of the morning seminar for prelunch martinis at the Ritz-Carlton Hotel. In 1960 she saw the publication of her collection of poems, *Colossus,* and also suffered through the breakup of her marriage. She committed suicide on February 10, 1963 and she, and her last book of poems, *Ariel,* have been the subject of extensive commentary and discussion ever since.

In his biography, which is an attempt to provide an overall interpretation of Sylvia Plath's life, Butscher, taking his clue from indications that Sylvia Plath had been fascinated with the problem of split personalities ever since she wrote her thesis for her bachelor's degree at Smith, turns this right around and applies it to his study of Sylvia herself. The face she showed to the world, he claims, was of a bright, modest, dutiful, hard-working efficient child of middle-class parents dedicated to strict Calvinist values and thankful for the slightest favors. Inwardly, Butscher argues, she was raging at the thought of her every humiliation—real or imagined. She suffered, he says, from "a neurotic fury that surfaced whenever her ego seemed violated and she felt forced to endure a dependent relationship with a lesser figure because of some external circumstances."

Butscher sees that rage as surfacing in *The Bell Jar* wherein she lashed out at everyone who had helped her, that is everyone who had in some way placed her under some kind of obligation. She is very bitter, for example, in her portrayal of the Brookline, Massachusetts, author who had set up a foundation on which Sylvia attended Smith. She is also very unkind in her slightly disguised picture of a Christian Scientist mother who had provided Sylvia with a summer job out on Cape Cod caring for her children.

When *The Bell Jar* was published, Sylvia's mother wrote to the publisher, Harper & Row, in an attempt to explain what she thought Sylvia had been trying to do in terms which would make her daughter's ingratitude more acceptable. "Practically every character in *The Bell Jar,*" the mother wrote, "represents someone—often in caricature—whom Sylvia loved; each person had given freely of time, thought, affection, and, in one case, financial help during those agonizing six months of breakdown in 1953."

Sylvia herself, on the other hand, had written her mother, "What I've done is to throw together events from my own life, fictionalizing to add color—it is a pot boiler really, but I think it will show how isolated a person feels when she is suffering a breakdown ... I've tried to picture my world and the people in it as seen through the distorting lens of a bell jar." But Butscher sees it as the suppressed side of Sylvia breaking out, going on a rampage of destruction, against those who had what she didn't—money, position—and who had, in some way, been able to make her cater to them.

Some sort of confirmation of this interpretation is to be found in Peter Davison's autobiography, *Half Remembered,* who recalls "Soon after settling into Cambridge I got in touch with an attractive blond girl named Sylvia Plath, whom I had met twice at Smith College the previous spring through Alfred Kazin. She had been writing poems and stories as well as a thesis on 'the double' in Dostoevsky ... I asked her to have dinner with me a few days later. She arrived in a white dress, with a deep suntan and thick hair turned blonder by the sun. She asked more and more questions, she seemed strangely elevated, and she hardly waited to be asked to slip into my new bed." A Mrs. Belmont might ask—Where's the reticence there?

He sums up his impression of Sylvia Plath this way: "To use experience is of course the way of artists, but I have encountered very few who grasped fellow humans quite so inhumanly as Sylvia did then. As Alfred Kazin wrote of her recently, 'The world existed just to be written about.'"

Of some people, like Sylvia Plath, biographers seem to think that they lived just to be written about. The biographers of Harry Crosby, John Marquand, Sylvia Plath, treat their subjects with a frankness which represents a great change over the discretion of a generation ago. Current biography sometimes seems to have taken as its epigraph Charles Baudelaire's frequently quoted line "Hypocrite lecteur—mon semblable, mon frere," and to suggest that there is no distinction without clay feet.

5

From John Marquand
to John Updike

From Newburyport, Massachusetts, where John Marquand wrote
some of his best-remembered novels in the late thirties and forties, to Ipswich, Massachusetts, where John Updike wrote the
novels which have supported claims for his being considered a
major American writer in the sixties, is but a few hundred wing
flaps as the crow flies. But the differences between Marquand's
Wickford Point of 1939, with its disguised Newburyport setting,
and Updike's *Couples* of 1968, with its relocated Ipswich setting,
are numerous and great. In those thirty years, the novel recorded
greater changes in style, characterization, and content than it ever
had in a hundred years previously. Some readers felt the form
had become offensive and irrelevant; others that, at last, it was
catching up with Manhattan or suburbia.

Few currently practicing critics are not embarrassed at the
memory of an angry piece, dashed off in an irritated moment
during the last twenty years, grumbling over the passing of the
novel. Few publishers, on the other hand, have not enjoyed themselves immensely, addressing an annual convention or an awards
dinner marking the success of one of their novels, reminding the
audience that the novel is alive and well, selling paperback versions in larger quantities than ever before, and earning for its
publishers reprint rights or movie rights or television rights in figures intelligible only to those who compute the national debt.

One of the reasons for this quasi immortality of the novel is
that, like a mythical Spenserian dragon, lop off one head and it
immediately grows another. Back in the fifties, when some of
Marquand's stuff was looked upon as risqué and adventuresome,
every Sunday *New York Times Book Review* carried column-long
reviews of new historical novels. That subspecies was pronounced

extinct in the early sixties when black humor was pronounced
more relevant by new cultural pundits and the nation's agonies
over Vietnam were supposed to preempt any concern with the
past. But, surprise, in the mid-seventies, the costume romance
was alive again in the form of torrid sex adventures in Istanbul
harems or New Orleans barracoons. The greatest money-makers
were a group of ladies writing for a Hearst publishing house,
Avon, about miscegenation in the Caribbean, flaggelation in
Paris, and confrontations between founders of the Republic like
Jefferson and their quadroon bedmates like Sally Hemmings.
Supermarket shoppers grabbed these limp-backed books off the
racks the way they did Wonder bread off the shelves. Both bread
and novel seemed necessary or relevant to a group of readers
those preoccupied with social significance had attempted to
divert or neglect.

Any attempt to capsulize the history of the novel during the last
thirty years would be foolish, beyond the attempts of Hercules to
confine Proteus. But there is one species of novel which can be
identified, tagged, isolated, and which seems to be especially
worth considering because it may serve as a more reliable index to
changes in taste than any other species. It is the novel of social
realism.

The label is Albert Guerard's in his recently published *Triumph
of the Novel,* where he traces the rise of this kind of novel from its
beginnings with Dickens to its decline with Faulkner.

Reviewing the rise and fall of the novel of social realism from
the point of view of Professor Guerard, noticing only its most distinguished practitioners, one might be tempted to think of
Faulkner who "came near what may turn out to have been its vir-
tual end." Looking at the rise and fall of the novel of social realism
only from the highlands, paying attention only to the peaks, one
might be tempted to accept Faulkner as its last act. But, taking into
consideration lesser artists, writers who might imitate or parody
the greater, writers who might probe the corners left unchecked
by the momentum of greater talents, that form still manifested
some vitality, and some of its lesser talents still illuminated, sometimes ironically sometimes directly, the segments of a society with
which they were particularly familiar.

John Marquand's *Late George Apley, Wickford Point,* and *Point of No
Return,* novels of the thirties and forties, were blurbed and read as
making insightful statements about the social conventions of

those days. John Updike in *Couples*, published in 1968, was reviewed as commenting on the social mores of the country a generation later.

In his *Memories and Milestones* (1915), John Jay Chapman, a perceptive and proper Bostonian who should be better known, recalled Martin Brimmer, who, in the opinion of many, came close to exemplifying the true Boston brahmin. Chapman particularly noted an exchange between himself and Brimmer which he thought came close to summing up the values that preoccupied Bostonians. According to Brimmer, as reported by Chapman, "the great business of Bostonians was to place values upon everything in the world with conscientious accuracy." Brimmer continued, "Professor Norton once said to me, on the steps of Sanders theater, after a performance of Beethoven's Eroica Symphony, that, after all, the 'sentiment of the funeral march was a little forced.'" This, for Chapman, was "an illustration of Boston's foible to set metes and bounds to everything: that was the game which we played; but it was a good game, and the players were among the best-hearted people in the world."

Marquand's George Apley was a Bostonian, a character not so much trying to set values on everything because the values with which he was concerned had been well reconnoitered by the time he is portrayed as arriving on the scene, but as a character trying to preserve those values. He is defined as a man living with a portfolio of charts ready at hand to help him identify landmarks: Freud cannot possibly be credited with the authority of an Emerson, a daughter's infatuation with a college tutor, and a son's affair with a Worcester girl—these do not fall within the explored conventions, so he sets about trying to bring the offspring within the boundaries of tradition.

In the 1930s, the late George, discoursing on things as they were twenty years before, seemed like an antediluvian holdover. He looked forward to holidays like Thanksgiving the way a medieval monk did to Easter. Each season's rites were to him prescribed by a social calendar as fixed as a Llandlaff abbot's by a liturgical calculation. George's life was right when things were as they had been, so at the groom's dinner, he gives way to tears at the singing of "Auld Lang Syne." This "sign of emotion" was received by the like-minded and the liberated who didn't dare do otherwise "with hearty applause." Through all the conflicts George persisted in believing a sentiment which, while true in 1912, was still not without many adherents in 1939, that "the family is more important than the individual and the family must be solid before the world, no matter what the faults of the individual."

John Marquand may not have been the most significant of the novelists writing in the late thirties and dealing with social questions—one thinks immediately of Faulkner and Steinbeck—but he was among the most popular. His style was slick and his subjects make him more relevant than many others might be to an exploration of the changes in taste coming over the city of Boston. In *The Late George Apley*, his satire is farcical with broad strokes caricaturing George's concern with bird-watching, the location of graves in the family cemetery plot, while unaware of the way the world is passing him by. With his 1912 attitudes, Apley was as vulnerable in 1936 as Malvolio in *Twelfth Night* reappearing in his yellow, cross-gartered medieval stockings.

In *Wickford Point* (1939), Marquand's satire is much more surgical, much more personal. The focus is on the Brill family as they are seen through the eyes of a Jim Calder, a cousin, who went to live with them when his mother died. Calder is a writer of serials for a magazine that clearly resembles the *Saturday Evening Post* of those days. Marquand, like Calder, was a regular *Post* writer, known especially for his detective stories featuring a Japanese Mr. Moto, before his success with *Apley*. In real life the Brills were Marquand's own relatives, the Hales, and Wickford Point was really the family estate in Newburyport. Since many of the characters in the novel could be readily identified with their real-life counterparts, Marquand was always worried that he might be sued for some of his more bitter shots. When Marquand became involved in a legal battle with the family in his quest to acquire the family property, the Hales gave interviews to *Life* magazine and quite affably identified the characters in the novel modeled after them. As Jim Calder, Marquand tried to put some distance between himself and his relatives. He seemed anxious to make sure the world would recognize that he had succeeded not with the help of his properly connected family but in spite of it. This is the way he put it: "Wickford Point could work no magic for me out where I was going. It was no shield to my inferiority, because I did not possess the imagination to romanticize it. I felt that I was different, but unlike the Brills this knowledge gave me no sense of careless ease, and I was never able to use it as an adequate excuse for failure."

And failure is what he studies in the Brills. There is Sid Brill, supposedly derived from Marquand's cousin, Robert Hale, who is pictured as a lazy, ne'er-do-well, a hypochondriac, and inclined to siphon gas out of anybody's tank to get to town. Then there is Harry Brill, based on Dudley Hale, a dreamer, who loves gossip and traffics on the family name. Also there is Belle, the beauty of the family who has left a trail of broken hearts, failed marriages, and hurt feelings behind her because she uses people to get just what she wants. Then there is Allen Sotheby, Belle's current victim, a Harvard professor, who is completely taken in by Belle and her family. He is eager to marry her and to edit the family papers.

There is no positive norm implied in Marquand's satire. He holds up the assemblage to barbed inspection but does not suggest some better point of view which would have improved their lives or the reader's. As familiarity with the kind of life pictured in *The Late George Apley* and *Wickford Point* faded, Marquand's cartoon-like distortions lost their point.

Another practitioner of this kind of social satire with a style more graceful, a meticulous eye for detail, and a finer sense of narrative structure was John O'Hara. As Marquand tended to set his scenes in New England settings, O'Hara's readers soon became familiar with a suburb which was suspiciously like Princeton, New Jersey, where O'Hara lived. The difference between a Boston suburb and a New York suburb as pictured by Marquand or O'Hara was much greater than the geographical distance separating them. Between Marquand's *Wickford Point* of 1939 and John O'Hara's *Ten North Frederick* of 1955, much had happened to the country, especially in attitudes toward sexual behavior, and much of it had been summarized by the publication of what was popularly known as the Kinsey report. Some people delighted in quoting what they thought were interesting statistics about extraordinary sexual performance, but these would have had little influence on social behavior. What did have a very strong impact on the way people behaved and believed was the Kinsey report's constant pointing to the difference between the way in which people professed allegiance to a moral code and the way in which they actually behaved. Novelists who had been exposing hypocrisy for years now found themselves without their standard theme. Hypocrisy was not occasional, it was common. Consequently, they felt free to expose it as it was.

In O'Hara's *Ten North Frederick,* Edith Chapin, mourning the death of her seemingly quite proper husband in a very proper way in a very correct house on a very correct address, is led by one loose end or another to recall the past, and readers get a look behind the imposing white door and the seldom-washed fanlight above. Her thirty-two-year-old son and forty-year-old daughter, in their bibulous and disrespectful behavior toward their mother and her friends at their father's funeral, prepare us for the revelations about Gibbsville-Princeton that occupy the entire novel. Where Marquand could make his characters seem sort of foolish for persisting in eccentric ways while clinging to older values, O'Hara's characters are frank hedonists, traveling much lighter, without encumbrances from the past. Irritated by daughter Ann's behavior toward the mourners who had come to the house after the church service, mother Edith gets involved in a conversation which dredges up memories of the past when she and her husband had prevented Ann from marrying as she wished.

"I know. I understand the irony in your voice. You still think we ruined your life, or you like to think that. But you must know when you're being honest with yourself that a marriage with an Italian boy in a jazz band wouldn't have lasted a year."

"If you had let me have the baby, if you and Father had given the marriage a chance. Done half as much to help it as you did to stop it."

"The baby was out of the question Ann. A baby five months after you married? How would the child itself explain that in later life? On legal documents, where you have to put down the date of your parents' marriage? To say nothing of your own friends, and for that matter, the father's friends. You know people of that—class—are just as conservative as the more well-to-do, if not more so."

Ann got up and went to the window. "The last time we talked about this we ended up having a very stormy scene."

"Yes, and you went away and didn't write me for months."

Mother and daughter are self-assured, self-possessed without manifesting any twinges of conscience over any moral issues. Discretion is the rule of the house, and self-indulgence is a matter of convenience and opportunity. O'Hara's people are quite different from Marquand's, and the differences between them are a reflection of the changes which had come over art and public taste between the forties and fifties.

The morals of this community were set, officially and unofficially, by the judge. Gibbsville's judge is Lloyd Williams, "a calculating man," whose dress, "in an era of double-breasted suits and real or imitation hand-painted neckties, was conspicuously inconspicuous." His ability to drink was "a political asset; he was a man, not a hypocrite, and another part of the asset was his reputation for being quite a man with the women." The judge was never caught doing anything wrong, but he was known to be a man who could be reasoned with. Here is a passage which describes the way he handles trivial matters. It gives some idea of how he could be "reasoned with" on greater matters.

The judge's car was parked free of charge in the lot across Lantenengo Street from the hotel. It was a small graft that the judge accepted as part of the honor of being a judge, and in using the lot as his downtown parking place he considered that he had bestowed an honor on the place. He did not accept free gasoline, oil, car washing, tires, flashlights or other goods and services. The fact that the judge used the lot was an endorsement and an advertisement, and a mutually satisfactory arrangement. The same space was always reserved for the judge, and he did not have to tip the boys. A pleasant greeting was all that was expected. (It was not likely that the owners would ever ask the judge for a major favor, but if they did he would take his custom elsewhere, and if he were to do that the owners would lose prestige. And, of course, it was possible that a telephone call from the judge might remind the police department that the parking-lot owners illegally obstructed sidewalk and street traffic throughout the day and part of the night. A judge is the only official who is universally feared by police officers; the only official who can give them orders and even make fools of them with impunity, and at the same time remain vaguely on their side.)

So that's the way the system works in Gibbsville, and it will continue uninterrupted because it is supported by Bob Hooker, editor of the community paper, the *Standard*.

Very little indeed of Bob's professional effort was wasted. His newspaper enjoyed quiet subsidies from the Coal & Iron

Company and the Republican party war chest, which seldom
differed on policy, and when they did differ, the differences
were not irreconcilable. A citizen who wondered what kind of
cars Bob owned would not have to peer in his garage; he could
make his deductions from the advertising in the *Standard*. Bob
Hooker had learned his profession in the days when newspa-
permen were given passes on railroads. As editor and publisher
he felt entitled to appropriate courtesies from hotels, steam-
ship lines, and any other enterprises that valued the good-will
of the press ... He knew something about mark-ups, and when
his wife bought a dress or a suit or a furry item, he paid
approximately the cost price, not the wholesale price. The
small loss to the merchant in the difference between the cost
and the wholesale was also the difference between favorable
mention in the *Standard*'s society column and no mention at all.
But such courtesy arrangements took place between the publisher and the principal. Any reporter who was caught "on the
take" was fired without warning. A bottle of whiskey or a box of
candy at Christmas was permissible; but greater courtesies
were restricted to the top level. "I want no grafters," Bob
Hooker would say to every new member of his staff.

Such was the moral tone set by the novel in the fifties. It really had
nothing to say, but it entertained readers with candid shots of
society, reminding them that this was the way things really were
and that any memories of seemingly better behavior had been
transmitted by resorting to hypocrisies.

People get bored looking at candid snapshots. The only people
who retain a prolonged interest are camera bugs who are
involved in the technicalities of the hobby and who have all kinds
of questions to ask about exposures, film speeds, and focal planes.
Their interest is less in the subject of the picture than in the
technique which made it possible to capture it on film. The
equivalent of the camera bug in the world of novel readers is the
university critic or his students who are familiar with problems of
shifting points of view, flashbacks, unreliable narrators. They can
become involved with a novel which has little to say but says it in a
very complex way.

In an extended essay in the *New York Review of Books* (July 15,
1976), Gore Vidal contrasted the extensive readership achieved

by the traditional novel and the shrinking group of readers interested in what he tagged the "university novel." Among the novels in this category he included John Barth's *Sot-Weed Factor,* William Gass's *Omensetter's Luck,* and Thomas Pynchon's *V* and *Gravity's Rainbow.* Vidal called them "university novels" because many of the writers of this kind of novel (not Pynchon) were on university faculties and the audiences which seemed most appreciative of their works were university audiences. Only these audiences could be expected to recognize Pynchon's wide-ranging philosophical references or to puzzle out some of Barth's multiple points of view. Vidal believed that this kind of novel would never reach the wide audience he had been addressing with some of his recent work like the best-selling recreation of the life of Aaron Burr, *Burr.*

One novelist, perhaps the exception that is always said to prove the rule, who had been winning the critical approval of university groups as well as reaching a wide audience was John Updike. His *Couples* (1968) was firmly within the tradition of the novel of social realism, but it was as dazzling as any university novel in its construction, symbolism, and felicities of style. It was a big, ambitious work linking the lives of ten couples in Tarbox, a fictitious town supposedly some twenty-two miles southeast of Boston, though not entirely unlike Ipswich, which is about that distance northeast of Boston and is where Updike was living at the time. The couples are mostly in their mid-thirties, and most of them have children. At the center of the novel is Piet Hanema, a building contractor, married to Angela, and they have two children. At the opening of the novel Piet is having an affair with Georgene Thorne, whose husband, Freddy, is the dentist in Tarbox, and at the numerous parties the couples are always having he serves as playmaker, joke master, and Pied Piper of malevolence.

In *The Elements of John Updike* (1970), Alice and Kenneth Hamilton point to the central intent of the novel.

> Piet's relationship with Georgene Thorne at the beginning of the story illustrates the assumptions current among the couples, that they have escaped from the consequences of the Fall and have found their way back to Eden. When Piet first went with Georgene and raised the question of contraception, she asked him whether Angela did not use Enovid and laughingly said, *"Welcome to the post-pill paradise."* Here Updike, by putting

Georgene's words into italics and by repeating the phrase later in the book, follows his usual practice of giving the reader a clue to one of the central images. The belief that we can re-enter Paradise is equivalent to the conviction that life can be painless and that our acts carry no fatal consequences.

Most reviewers in the popular media did not dwell on this aspect of the novel but called attention to the numerous explicit sex scenes. They also noted the many similarities among the various characters making it difficult for the reader to keep them separate in his mind.

Of the seriousness of Updike's purpose, no sensitive reader could have had any doubt. He did want to take sex out of the closet and to show that the hope of finding in it an answer to all problems was going to prove disappointing. His characters, for all their preoccupations with sex, sense this ultimate exhaustion, and they cling together desperately hoping they will find an answer. They are like members of a church with a secular ritual, no dogma and no real hope. Angela, when discussing with her husband, Piet, the behavior of their group, recalls some of the remarks Freddy Thorne the dentist has made about them. She says: "He thinks we're a circle. A magic circle of heads to keep the night out. He told me he gets frightened if he doesn't see us over a weekend. He thinks we've made a church of each other."

When the couples, the congregation, get together for their services, which are usually Saturday evening parties, Freddy, with "his hyena appetite for dirty truths," encourages them to play guessing games wherein they hint to each other who is sleeping with whom and who is pregnant. The kind of gossip which seemingly sustains them is a parody of the charity and mutual concern of members of a true church. When they have to part at the termination of their games, usually on a Sunday afternoon, they experience sadness. They don't know what to do with themselves. One of the wives sums it up thus: "She was experiencing this chronic sadness of late Sunday afternoon, when the couples had exhausted their game, basketball or beachgoing or tennis or touch football, and saw an evening weighing upon them, an evening without a game, an evening spent among the flickering lamps and cranky children and leftover food."

Thorne, like some of the other members of his sect, has no great hopes. At one point, he tells the assembled couples: "In the western world there are only two comical things: the Christian church and naked women. We don't have Lenin so that's it. Everything else tells us we're dead." When Piet slips into Freddy's bed for his first coupling with Georgene, he finds Freddy has a collection of bedside pornography, and this is part of the background the reader has to recall when Freddy makes his definitive statement: "People are the only thing people have since God packed up. By people I mean sex." And of course Freddy has been and is being continually disappointed by sex.

Updike wanted to call attention to the sadness and emptiness of it all. Many thought he was exploiting sex. In general the impact of the novel was to leave the impression that society was more and more openly indulging in sex games and that novels were more and more erotic, leaving both society and the novel with nowhere to go.

That of course was not true. It is possible to trace a further decline in zest and sensibility from a character like Freddy Thorne of *Couples* to Bill Slocum, the corporation man of vague obligations but affluent way of living who is the central figure of Joseph Heller's *Something Happened* (1974). Bill is a thoroughly frustrated man at work, curbing all his anger against his job and against his superiors, but taking it out on his family at home. Sadly, he is still capable of caring, and he claims he cares especially for his nine-year-old son, but this caring for his son is less a concern for the child than a reflection of his anxieties about himself. When, toward the very end of a novel in which very little happens, he attempts to comfort the boy after an accident, he actually crushes the child to death.

Slocum is a man several rungs lower than the *Couples'* men on the ladder down to absolute despair. For him there is no church of the like-minded with whom he can play temporarily diverting games. He is a man turned inward, upon himself and he uses everybody about him to provide some temporary relief from the blackness of the pit.

When I see my wife or children doing something improper, or making a mistake for which I know I will be justified in blaming them, I do not intercede to help or correct, but hold back in joy to watch and wait, as though observing from a distance a wicked scene unfold in some weird dream, actually relishing the opportunity I spy approaching that will enable me to criticize and reprimand them and demand explanations and apologies.

These temporary sadistic pleasures of Bill Slocum are not relieved by any wild bedroom caperings, for he experiences no joy in sex. His participation in the sex game is because of its importance in the seeking of status. Were it not for a reputation he feels he must maintain at the office of being successful in the pursuit of women, and also to reassure himself from time to time, he would not engage in what are really just compulsive seductions. He would not, as he says, "give orgasms to any of them."

These moments of compromise leave Slocum with a realization that he is vulnerable. He knows other people are and it is his game to exploit their vulnerability. Beneath it all he is a pitiful creature and he senses it: "God damnit—I want to be treated like a baby sometimes by my wife and kids. I've got a right. I'm not one of those parents that expect to be taken care of by their children in their old age. I want my children to take care of me now."

For the Slocums of this world there can be little hope. Life has reached a dead end in narcissistic dependency. The university novelists, making no attempt to provide substantive answers, provide diversions in the form of superb stylistic tricks. John Barth, best known for his *Sot-Weed Factor* and *Giles Goat-Boy* suggests that escape for the Slocums is to be found in the development of a style, style in life for the worker, style in writing for the novelist. In *Vulnerable People,* a study of American fiction since 1945, Josephine Hendin sums up Barth's contributions to our self-understanding this way: "As Odysseus outwitted the Cyclops by claiming he was 'no man,' so Barth's people outwit adversity by denying or erasing everything but a wily voice … For his people, style is life-style, the logic of the sentence refutes the mind's chaos, syntax can be a saving grace and parody is the only force for order." So the less intellectual or moral baggage a man is carrying, the quicker he can adapt. Movement is the only hope and satisfaction is catching a glimpse of oneself doing it with style.

For Barth the self is fabricated, a work each creates not for but of himself, and the main way is through a skillful use of parody. The present self is never to be taken seriously because it is not permanent; it may have to be abandoned this week or next. Discovery is a perception of vulnerability, and knowing one's vulnerability will enable one to build the defenses higher. But no one should be fooled. There is no happiness to be found behind the bulwarks of a parody that must be abandoned sooner or later. The happy man is the ironist, Hamlet bitterly explaining to Horatio that his mother's marriage followed fast upon his father's funeral because they wanted to be thrifty, to use the food baked and left over from the wake at the wedding. So the device Hamlet used to protect himself and disguise his deepest hurt has now become the posture of self-preservation.

Donald Barthelme, another novelist with more readers in academia than in the marketplace, is also constantly portraying the gloom consequent upon any sober reflection on life. One of his widely discussed *New Yorker* stories later incorporated in a collection, *The Glass Mountain,* is a parody of an old fable about a youth determined to climb a high mountain to free a beautiful princess imprisoned at the top. In Barthelme's version, the mountain becomes an Eighth Avenue, New York, all-glass skyscraper. The hero sets out to climb the outside to get to the top where there is a symbol of beauty he wishes to contemplate close up.

All the way up, as he climbs, the young man, that is, the artist in quest of beauty, is threatened and reviled by the people looking up and expecting him to fall any minute as many others who have tried it have fallen. This suggests what Barthelme thinks about the masses. When the climber does get to the top, he is disappointed. His symbol of beauty turns out to be "only a beautiful princess." So he flings her down the building to the crowd below who can be expected to know what to do with her. Moral of the story—there is no beauty at the top of the mountain; there is nothing but hatred in the people and depression in the artist. Technically the construction of the story and the adaptation of the myth are brilliant.

The most fashionable of the academic cults of the novel at the moment is of the works of Thomas Pynchon who is reported to have rejected the ultimate accolade, a *Time* magazine cover story. His *V* and *Gravity's Rainbow* are large works which incorporate large sections of our culture, including many aspects of current science, which he does better than any other of these novelists. Man is portrayed as the victim of this science and culture, but he is flawed in every way. All of man's seemingly noble emotions are portrayed as self-interested and suspect. There seem to be only two directions to go: toward achieving complete sensitivity or toward giving up completely. Pynchon seems to tend toward the latter alternative. He concludes his latest, *Gravity's Rainbow,* with the statement: "Our mission is to promote death." His message seems to be an extrapolation of those French decadents like Huysmans or the Russian khlists who preached that the road to sainthood lay through utter degradation. Until man discovered how low he could sink through every kind of self-indulgence, he could not hope to find the strength through humility to rise again.

So Pynchon preaches we should mistrust everything—art, sex, reason—and his vision is the most pessimistic. Some of his admirers argue that this is a reflection of his intense caring about humanity, the proof of his belief in our power to recover if we will only give up the traps that have caged us. His statement, however, is unquestionably very negative, a logical conclusion of a process well under way when Marquand was satirizing Apley's beliefs. What began with poking fun at conventions that had lost their underlying support thirty years ago and were just empty ceremonials has ended up with stronger and stronger statements that there is nothing that can serve as a basis for belief, for the erection of new ceremonials symbolic of an existential center.

Post–World War II fiction has been satirical, negative, technically accomplished, with an insistent emphasis on human limitations. Earlier fiction had portrayed man as capable of building, creating, doing some good, establishing some order. In the recent fiction man deludes himself if he thinks he can organize experience, except verbally, or control any part of it, except temporarily. What current fiction encourages is a kind of detachment, an achievement of invulnerability by dropping out or not getting involved or not caring. So the hero has become the laid-back, cool cat, the drifter, who knows he is vulnerable but uses his vulnerability to manipulate others and, the one satisfaction, makes sure he is not used himself by keeping people distant through parody.

The yearning for something more encouraging to read about is reflected in the recent success of paperback historical novels and costume romances. Signs of a reaction setting in can also be found in some recent criticism. In *On Moral Fiction,* John Gardner states his dissatisfaction in terms so explicit neither academia nor the general reader can fail to understand: "In a world where nearly everything that passes for art is tinny and commercial, and often, in addition, hollow and academic, I argue for an old-fashioned view of what art is and does and what the fundamental business of critics ought therefore to be." What he is arguing for ought to be known to anyone who has ever read—or heard about—Homer, Plato, Aristotle, Dante, and the rest of what used to be called the "western tradition," but Gardner, like many others, has found that his former orthodoxy has now become strange to university lecture goers and late-night academic discussions. He sums up his view of what fiction should try to be thus:

> The traditional view is that true art is moral; it seeks to improve life, not debase it. It seeks to hold off, at least for a while, the twilight of the gods and us. I do not deny that art, like criticism, may legitimately celebrate the trifling. It may joke, or mock, or while away the time. But trivial art has no meaning or value except in the shadow of more serious art, the kind of art that beats back the monsters and, if you will, makes the world safe for triviality. That art which tends towards destruction, the art of nihilists, cynics, and merdistes, is not properly art at all. Art is essentially serious and beneficial, a game played against chance and death, against entropy. It is a tragic game, for those who have the wit to take it seriously, because our side must lose; a comic game—or so a troll might say—because only a clown with sawdust brains would take our side and eagerly join in.

In *October Light,* a novel by John Gardner published in 1976, we have a bit of an illustration of the kind of novel which he thinks has something to say about integrity, about people who believe in their ideas, who look upon life as something to be lived, not suffered. This is the story of a tragicomic conflict that develops between Sally Paige, an eighty-three-year-old feminist, and James, her seventy-year-old brother, when they are forced to share the old family homestead on a Vermont farm. James is devoted to the land and the satisfactions and the rhythms of farming. Sally is devoted to the fascinating world that television has brought to the farm. She spends her days watching television; James spends his days doing the chores. The clash between the two value systems and personalities reaches a climax when James, unable to bear any more of the television's noise, shoots the set with his deer rifle and Sally rushes up to her room. She locks herself in and proceeds to hold out against James's arguments and blandishments.

Both are immovable, in a way which Emerson and George Apley would have admired, where their values are concerned. Both are convinced that they are right. Gardner portrays both sides with equal authority. Who should win? neither? both? The answer suggested seems to be that it doesn't matter. The only losers are those with nothing to stand for. There is only one failure, lack of commitment.

For Gardner right living is not so much a moral problem as a logical problem. What is to be avoided is the excluded middle, the ambivalent term which, when taken in different senses, leads to fallacious inferences. People like James and Sally, committed to the point where they are willing to perform the kinds of actions which the French existentialists like Sartre and Camus thought gave meaning to existence, seem like dinosaurs, prehistoric creatures, in the midst of other novel creations which are parodies of anything to get a giggle out of the reader. Gardner is as serious as his creations. No more hit and run with broad farcical strokes like Marquand. Art, like life, is serious. Art should illuminate life, not just live off it like some of the Brills in *Wickford Point*—and Marquand in his novels.

The whirligig of taste has come full circle in Boston since the time when Marquand could poke fun at the late George because he stuck by things which no longer seemed to matter. The late George was no James Paige. George was much more articulate, polished. He didn't have to fight for his ideas; he could become sentimental to the point of tears over them. James Paige can't articulate his beliefs as well as his sister—or George Apley. But he senses what he believes is right and being threatened. Gardner is articulating what a lot of people like James Paige have been sensing they were missing for some time. Gardner hasn't taken the next step yet. It will require the definition of a system of values which support the positions of both Sally and James. It would require going back to a point before the Apleys came on the scene, not necessarily to revive the Victorian system of values which, after all, only led to a kind of failure, but to try to do better than the Victorians did, to define a better system of beliefs to support ideas and a more than temporary style of living, to support a life-style, a much abused word, which would be predicted to have a half-life longer than temporary parody.

6

From *Ward Eight* to
The Friends of Eddie Coyle

When Abraham Lincoln was introduced to Harriet Beecher Stowe, his first remark is reported to have been, "So you're the little woman who wrote the book that made this great war." If we are to take Lincoln's reported assessment of the effect of *Uncle Tom's Cabin,* we would have to consider it one of the most influential books in history. As such it could serve as an archetype of the political novel at least as it is defined by Gordon Milne in *The American Political Novel.* He includes in this genre "novels illustrating a conflict between two ideologies such as communism and democracy, or novels examining the connection between the political figure and the body politic...Just as political discussion is apt to be heated, so is a political novel. The best ones, well, even the worst, generate considerable passion, bringing their ideas to life, stirring the reader's emotions, and provoking controversy."

Stir emotions and provoke controversy, *Uncle Tom's Cabin* certainly did. So also did John Steinbeck's *Grapes of Wrath* (1939) with its portrayal of the treatment and displacement of the Oklahoma farmers during the bottom of the depression into the migrant "Okies." Not all political novels attempt to rouse passions like these. Many more seem to concentrate on that other part of Milne's definition by portraying the conflict between two ideologies or examining the connection between the political figure and the body politic.

The earliest novel written mainly about Boston politics and by a Bostonian recorded in Joseph Blotner's *The Modern American Political Novel* (1966) and intended to show the connection between the political figure and the body politic was Joseph Dineen's *Ward Eight.* Written in 1939 it is mainly concerned with events that occurred in Boston from as early as 1890 and ends with references to ethnic shifts that took place in the mid-1920s. The title is taken from the number of the Boston city ward which included the streets around the old North Church and Copp's Hill. When the story starts, the Irish are just beginning to take over the territory. When the story ends, the Irish have just about moved out and the Italians are taking over, beginning another cycle. There are many reflective passages in the novel which indicate that the author was concerned with the implications of the cycle of change: "An entire Irish population had moved into the ward and crowded out an entire Yankee population ... Another cycle was casting its shadow before it."

But *Ward Eight* is less about the cycles in population and political change than it is a study of two political figures: the ward boss and the young reformer. The boss is Hughie Donnelly and the young reformer is his understudy and challenger Tim O'Flaherty. The political novel which focused on the big city boss was a recurring type that reached its peak, in its study of Boston politics at least, in Edwin O'Connor's *Last Hurrah.* The political novel which focused on a young reformer was also an established type, the clearest instance concerned with Boston politics was Harry Sylvester's *Moon Gaffney.* Joseph Dineen in *Ward Eight,* in trying to combine the two, attempted too much.

The young reformer plot in *Ward Eight* centers around Tim O'Flaherty, known as "Big Tim" because of his size. As a youngster he is everything required of a Horatio Alger stereotype: up early, off on his paper route; dedicated to his mother to whom he turns over all his earnings; slow to anger; a tiger provoked. He distinguishes himself in his studies not so much because of his brilliance as his application, and he forges new paths for the Irish kids in the neighborhood, going on not only to high school but to Boston College and law school. He is helped along by the Boss but always tries to be his own man.

The crisis comes when Big Tim has an opportunity to stand for election on his own as a reformer, opposing the Boss's machine. A standard scene in political novels and movies is the conversation which takes place between Big Tim and Ann Barrett, a Beacon Hill type who has set up a family counseling service in the Irish ward. She is trying to save Tim by finding the Yankee money to support him.

"You've come a long way, Tim," she went on thoughtfully. "Now you're in sight of the goal. You'll be elected, if not this year, another year. You'll beat Hughie and liberate his slaves. You can clean up the ward then, Tim, put a stop to all this petty graft and corruption, lift the burden of fear from every home in the ward. You can make honest men of them. You can..."

Big Tim's brow had been clouding. "You're not actually suggesting that I become a reformer?" he asked.

...[a reformer's] "as bad down here as an *informer,* and as cordially hated. If I don't ultimately take over Hughie's organization, I'll have to build one of my own. I can't change the system single-handed. It would be political suicide for me to try. All I can do is accept it and make the most of it."

..."I couldn't be a reformer. It seems so futile for me to stand alone against them all in an idealistic movement that would guarantee my downfall in politics."

She stood up. "The day may come, Tim, when you'd rather have had that honorable downfall than the success you may have following in Hughie's footsteps."

There we have the young tormented Lincolnesque figure. He would like to fight corruption without compromise. He sees his political commitments as a reflection of his religious convictions and would like to right all evils, but matters never work out that neatly. As the conscientious reformer, he is a fictional adaptation of the real-life reformers and muckrakers, writers like Upton Sinclair, Lincoln Steffens, Ida Tarbell, especially the last who, in a series of articles published in *McClure's Magazine* between 1902 and 1904, had exposed the corruption of Standard Oil and other monopolies. They encouraged young men to dream of devoting their lives to cleaning up corruption. They went into politics as young knights, on emotional as much as intellectual grounds, and they usually ended fighting for the good because of some woman.

Ward Eight is not a good illustration of this kind of novel for the Big Tim story is intertwined with the story of the Boss Hughie's. A better illustration of the kind of political novel which focuses more sharply on a young dragon slayer is Harry Sylvester's *Moon Gaffney* (1947). The scene is New York, not Boston. Moon is a young lawyer working for Tammany when he decides that Tammany Hall is not the primary source of evil in the New York of the 1930s but the Catholic Church because of its anti-labor stance and its many reactionary clerics. Moon's stand eventually costs him his job, and he finds himself down to defending cases no one else wants, like that of three dockworker union members. He is told that they are black and that one is a Communist. One of his concluding remarks is, "I knew that was coming sooner or later," but he continues unflinching, uncorrupted. The novel was one of the first to explore the labor and black problems, and excited many young Boston Catholic intellectuals in the late forties and fifties.

The character who dominates Joseph Dineen's *Ward Eight* is Hughie Donnelly, the boss of the ward. Since the novel was followed some ten years later, 1946, by the publication of another study of a political boss, Robert Penn Warren's *All the King's Men*, a readily recognized fictional treatment of the shenanigans of Louisiana's imperial governor of the thirties, Hughie Long, and ten years after that by Edwin O'Connor's *Last Hurrah*, generally accepted as based on Boston's political boss, James Michael Curley, the political novel built around a big city boss's manipulation of municipal affairs for his own gain was commonly thought to be a new kind of book. Actually it was far from that, for back in 1901 Francis Churchill Williams had published *J. Devlin, Boss*, which reflected corruption in city politics going all the way back to the Grant administration. All the characteristics that came to be associated with the portrayal of the boss in the later novels are there, though the forces that were responsible for the boss's power are portrayed only in the most superficial of terms.

Devlin, the boss, and his saloon-keeping friend, Kennedy, are pictured as having gained control of Tammany Hall, and, thereby, of New York politics. Although they are enriching themselves by manipulating city franchises, they look upon this as honest graft, whereas they have nothing but contempt for the Wall Street manipulators whom they look upon as really stealing from the people. The people are held responsible for their own exploitation because they are too lazy to be concerned about good government. Old Mike, the saloon keeper's father, has watched them for years, and this is his advice for his son:

"Never interfere with people's beer; give 'em clean streets; double the number of lamp posts, an' have bands playin' in every pa-r-rk. Then kape th' street free of ba-ad people ... the public don't object to dirt, but it wants it kept in the back alleys. Jawn, if you'll follow what I tell you, you can do what else ye plaze."

Irish politicians supposedly spoke like that back in 1901 and though the attempts at dialect may be unconvincing, the estimation of the public is familiar.

Some thirty years later, Harold Zink, in *City Bosses in the United States,* compiled a list of characteristics which he had found common to twenty municipal bosses he had studied. Fictional boss J. Devlin had some of them, but Hughie Donnelly had them all. Like the real-life bosses of Zink's study, Hughie of *Ward Eight* was urban-born of impoverished foreign-born parents. Like half of the city bosses studied, he was Irish; half were practicing Roman Catholics, so was Hughie. They all had had to go to work prematurely, usually because of the death of a father, and so had Hughie. Their path through politics had been the same; they entered young, learned its tricks the hard way, fought dirty, depended upon an organization for their office and power, amassed fortunes, and took care of their own. So the boss of the political novel was no more a stereotype than his real-life counterpart.

Hughie ruled the ward because he guaranteed his voters their livelihood. He was feared because he could deprive many a head of a household of his work for the city instantly. He could also be counted on to help by donating to all religious and charitable causes, to furnish bail for minor offenders, drunks, and bettors. He would appear in public only once a year for a grand social event, but if there was any real trouble in the ward—a near riot—his appearance would stop it right away. He was judge as well as provider, his word the last in any domestic matter brought before him.

After his attempted rebellion, Big Tim realizes he can't defeat Hughie, so he settles down to work for him as a member of his kitchen cabinet and as his representative in the state house where "oratory couldn't sway a single vote." Elected by Hughie to the city council, he works behind the facade of a reform mayor while Hughie continues to dispense contracts for favors received behind the scenes. Hughie has a justification for this that Big Tim comes to share:

> "I've been through a lot of business administrations before your time, Timmy, and I niver yet saw one that was popular with the great mass of the people after the first six months of it. They can say what they want to about the grafter. He may be as crooked as a corkscrew, but business is always good when the grafter is in office, and 'tis rotten when a business man runs the government ... The grafter has to spend money to make money. Ten dollars out of every hundred he spends may find its way into his pocket or into the pockets of the gang; but when you come to think of it, ten per cint isn't a bad charge for the handlin' of it. The bank gets more..."

With death imminent, Hughie gives Big Tim some last advice: "If ye're strong and crafty and fight hard and never quit, ye may be a boss in twenty years more, but yer hair'll be gray before ye're in command." Dineen implied that Big Tim's day would never come for he thought the day of the boss was over. For all his sympathetic portrayal of Hughie and the fine speeches he put in his mouth in justification of his taking ways, this is how he describes his death as seen through the eyes of a friend.

> "There was a look in his eye such as might burn in the eye of an old wolf that has crept away in solitude to die. I felt that I was in the presence of the oldest thing in the world—a thing more ancient than the sphinx or aged pyramids. This once Boss, silent and passive and white and old, waiting for the digging of his grave, is what breeders call a 'throwback.' In what should arm him for a war of life against life, he is a creature of utter cunning, utter courage, utter strength. He is a troglodyte; he is that original one who lived with the cave bear, the mastodon, the saber-toothed tiger, and the Irish elk."

The day of the troglodytes was not over, neither in fact nor fiction. In the year of 1976 Mayor Daley still ruled in Chicago as fictitious Hughie ruled in Boston.

The most successful of the studies of big-city bosses was still to come some twenty years later with the publication of Edwin

O'Connor's *Last Hurrah* in 1956. O'Connor also has a deathbed scene with a Monsignor standing by, having just heard the boss Frank Skeffington's last confession. He reflects: "Well, no matter what some of us may have thought in the past, it's all different now. And I think we can say this: that knowing what he knows now, if he had it all to do over again, there's not the slightest doubt but he'd do it all very, very differently."

At this point, Skeffington is portrayed as "raising himself slightly, his eyes were now wide open, and in them they saw the old challenging, mocking gleam. And they heard his voice, as taking charge now for the last time he gave his answer: 'The hell I would.'" To which the old Monsignor responds, "Oh grand, grand, grand..." And the reader is left with the feeling that he would like to echo that final sentiment. The ending, like all of the novel, leaves the reader with plenty of opportunities to see both the good and the bad sides of Skeffington and the system he worked within. But O'Connor also tells the story against the background of the social changes which had taken place in the thirties and forties, changes which had resulted in the federal government's providing those aids upon which the boss's power had been built: jobs and security.

The Last Hurrah is the story of seventy-two-year-old Francis Skeffington's last campaign in search of the mayoralty of Boston. Skeffington invites his skeptical nephew, political cartoonist Adam Caulfield, to accompany him on his vote-seeking rounds. Adam thus becomes a representative of the general reader as Skeffington thinks of himself "as the last of the old-style political leaders who's still alive and moving around."

Skeffington is like all the stereotyped real-life and fictional city bosses who had preceded him: forced on to the streets young, a quick study, an aggressive and persuasive Irishman. What distinguishes him is his oratory, which was also distinctive of James Michael Curley, mayor of Boston. O'Connor had the sharpest ear for the nuances in speech, and his re-creation of Boston characters and their conversations lifted a thrice-told tale from the level of the commonplace to that of the distinguished.

In his first campaign, Skeffington had won because his gift of gab had stirred the crowd, and he had gone on to develop the city's first slum clearance program and public health recreation program. But the opposition knows that Skeffington has been responsible for widespread theft and the padding of the public payrolls. So in his last campaign he is defeated by a bland young Irishman who is really fronting for a business crowd led by a power trust. Actually he loses because the federal government is now providing the social services the boss used to provide. Adam is told that Franklin D. Roosevelt "made the kind of politician your uncle was an anachronism, a sport over the country. The bosses have been dying for the last twenty years, uncle lasted this long simply because he was who he was; an enormously popular man whose followers were devoted to him ... the old boss was recognized simply because he held all the cards. What Roosevelt did was to take the handouts out of local hands. A few little things like Social Security, Unemployment Insurance, and the like."

The political novel with a strong boss figure at its center would not, however, ever be the same after O'Connor because his was such a superior blend of characterization and artistic insight that few would want to compete with it. O'Connor was incisive yet reverent; analytical yet comic; sympathetic yet critical. In effect he seemed to have succeeded in saying about the boss all that could be said in that form.

The political novels about the young reforming idealist and the city boss had one common characteristic. They were both centrally concerned with the portrayal of a character. There might be some discussion of the forces that were responsible for the character's success or failure. In Dineen's *Ward Eight* the explanation was sociological, the changes in ethnic voting patterns; in *The Last Hurrah* it was economical, the government's provisions for security. But the novel was held together not by its presentation of the operation of these forces but by its portrayal of the central character and his court or his enemies.

With the publication of *Let George Do It* (1957) by John Foster, commonly recognized as a pseudonym for a former governor of Massachusetts, Foster Furcolo, the focus shifted away from the character to a study of the system itself. In *The Modern American Political Novel,* Joseph Blotner comments: "On reflection, one cannot help thinking what a primer the book would make for the aspiring ward heeler if he could use it and manage to stay out of jail."

The course in practical politics an aspirant could take from *Let George Do It* would not be an advanced course. Most of the tricks mentioned are too crude to be effective today. To get Pete Martin elected, George Clancy decides he must be presented as an ethnic candidate appealing to all of Massachusetts' minority groups. So he has cards and signs printed up for Pietro Martino as well as Pierre Martin; he has messages read over the air, purportedly from Martin's Polish mother in Polish. These devices are but elaborations of the stories told about many a candidate, like Fiorello Laguardia running for mayor of New York and address-ing voting groups in Italian and Yiddish and letting each think he was one of them. The style of the novel also did not fit well with its subject, so that it's main interest for today, except for those who can identify all the real-life characters behind the fictional, is its heralding a shift, at least in novels about Boston politics, away from a concern with the man behind the political machine to an examination of the workings of the machine itself.

It may have been at this point that the American political novel could have gone on to concern itself, as the political novel had in Europe, with ideological conflicts more than with personalities and thus have extended the dimensions of its concerns. In *Writers of the Left,* Daniel Aaron raises the question why American novelists like Hemingway, Dreiser, and Lewis, who used political materials, did not, like European novelists Silone, Koestler, and Malraux, make them the central concerns of their novels. As a result he thinks American novels about politics were unable to approach true tragedy as many of the European novels did. "Was it possible," he asks, "that American writers were not 'close' to situations in which the ideological conflict makes for genuine tragedy? Were these 'ideological matters' entertained as abstrac-tions merely and not passionately felt?"

In the political novels about Boston, certainly ideological con-flicts were used only as background material with one possible exception, and that was in May Sarton's *Faithful Are the Wounds* (1955).

In *Faithful Are the Wounds*—the title taken from Proverbs 27: "Faithful are the wounds of a friend but the kisses of an enemy are deceitful"—Edward Cavan, a distinguished professor of Ameri-can Literature at Harvard, commits suicide. His sister Isabel comes east from California for the funeral and seeks to learn the details which led up to his death. Gradually she discovers that Cavan (commonly believed to stand for F.O. Matthiessen who taught at Harvard, had published *American Renaissance,* and com-mitted suicide in 1950) had recently broken with several of his friends over political issues, which he took very seriously.

He had parted with his departmental chairman because he had
refused to sign a statement to protest the firing of an economics
professor at the University of Nebraska who had campaigned for
Socialist Henry Wallace. He was embroiled in a fight with the
Boston chapter of the American Civil Liberties Union because it
seemed to him compromising its principles by furnishing its
national headquarters with a statement that no member of the
chapter was a Communist. He had fought with his life-long
friend, a professor of physics, for his willingness to supply the
national headquarters with the statement.

In short Edward Cavan was a person for whom politics mattered very much. He was an idealist, dedicated to a straightfor-
ward kind of socialism that manifested itself in his direct support
of the working man as well as gifts and lobbying for leftist causes.
He was increasingly out of step with the developing bureaucratic
socialism of the day, misunderstood, though admired, by his students, and reduced to one friendship with seventy-year-old Alice
Kimlock who was known for her extreme positions. The author
suggests that Cavan was never as effective politically in his life as
he became by the taking of it. His action made people think about
their own positions and what his loss meant for the community. In
that way the novel, nowhere as popular as the novels about the
bosses, was much more than a character study and approached, if
it did not achieve, tragic dimensions. It might have been much
more widely read if there had not been an epilogue which was a
bit preachy in its justification of Cavan, suggesting that in his
death and by his actions he had foreseen the coming of the
McCarthy Committee hearings in the 1950s. The novel also
portrays through various characters a wide range of liberal and
radical opinion. There is an archaic Socialist who echoes the
Darwinians and a slightly more up-to-date Socialist who is still
living, mentally, in the generation of G. B. Shaw. Then there is one
of Cavan's students who, it is suggested, with time will move to
take positions Cavan himself would have taken.

Looking back on novels that have been written with Boston
politics playing an important part since World War II, it is possible
to observe a progression, not too pronounced but admissible for
the purpose of imposing some clarity on the development. The
first, heirs of an earlier muckraking tradition, featured the young
idealist who was out to slay the last dragon. Then we had, with *The
Last Hurrah* and its Boston setting and Robert Penn Warren's *All*

the King's Men with its Louisiana setting, a concern with the boss and corruption of the machine. More recently we have had a series of novels which seem to accept corruption, detail it, and hold out little hope of ever eradicating it.

In George Higgins's *Judgment of Deke Hunter* (1976), we find ourselves observing a forty-year-old failed professional baseball player, now a state trooper, gathering evidence that the assistant district attorney of Middlesex County, Richard Shanley, will need to prosecute Teddy Donnelly, Leaper Donovan, and Andy Marr for robbing the Danvers National Bank of forty thousand dollars. He has to work with the lawyers, Sam Wyman, John Killelea, and other troopers like Horace Carmody. They all know how the system works and they all have reasons for being sour on life. They wisecrack about how the jury will behave, what will influence the judge, and what happens in jail. This crowd does not believe in law enforcement as much as it does in law adjustment. They are not out to do or die like the young idealists of earlier political novels, nor do they follow the dictates of some boss who can call all the shots. They are out for themselves and they try to protect themselves at all times. They know they have to deal with each other, to make deals with the opposition, so they are willing to listen to any reasonable compromise. In these novels, the game is much more interesting than the players. And the players only see part of the whole picture. The part they see, they claim they know well. They are the inside dopesters. Survival in the system is the only proof of being in the know.

In *Politics and the Novel,* Irving Howe suggested that "The criteria for evaluating a political novel must finally be the same as those for any other novel: how much of our life does it illuminate? how ample a moral vision does it suggest?—but these questions occur to us in a special context, in that atmosphere of political struggle which dominates modern life. For both the writer and the reader, the political novel provides a particularly severe test: politics rakes our passions as nothing else, and whatever we may consent to overlook in reading a novel, we react with an almost demonic rapidity to a detested political opinion."

Applying these criteria to these Boston political novels reveals that they were, for the most part, more interested in entertaining than illuminating a significant part of our lives. All were interesting in their character portrayals: *Ward Eight* in its suggesting the cycles of ethnic urban change as the prime political force in the

life of a city and *The Last Hurrah* in its outlining of the consequences of the growth of the federal bureaucracy. But only in
Faithful Are the Wounds was there a sustained attempt to engage the
reader in an emotional exploration of the moral dilemmas
resulting from political commitments. These novels did not
enrage as some political novels might because they did not engage
our political feelings . Politics provided the arena for the disposi-
tion of characters more than the development of theories or
ideas.

The year after these lectures were delivered witnessed the
publication of *Mortal Friends* by James Carroll, the book about
Boston politics intended to end all books on the subject. It was a
work in three parts. The first is set in Ireland during the 1916
Easter uprising and provides a background for an understanding
of the family loyalties that would be carried over to Boston by the
immigrants. The second has Colman Brady, the central figure in
the whole book and the survivor of the uprising, go through a
series of experiences as a member of the Curley organization very
similar to the experiences Dineen had Big Tim running through
as a member of Hughie's machine. The third is concerned with
Brady's attempts to ensure his son's national political career. In
this last section Brady is dealing with the Mafia and acting as a
front man for the kind of corrupt system which is portrayed in
Higgins novels like *The Friends of Eddie Coyle.* So within this one
book, *Mortal Friends,* were summed up most of the themes and
situations which had characterized some of the more famous
novels about Boston politics in the past. Surprisingly, *Mortal
Friends,* in spite of its having something for everybody, failed to
catch on. Reviews were lukewarm. Long-time Boston residents
kept pointing to factual mistakes in Boston history or descriptions
of localities. There was also a general feeling that there was little
interest now in reading about Boston bosses, ethnic neighbor-
hoods, or deals with the underworld. Readers were looking for
something new in political novels, and this novel wasn't it.

7

From *Peace of Mind* to TM

When publishers could return to printing books with wide margins without observing the restrictions on paper use imposed by rationing during World War II, the hardback novel once again became the star of the publishing world and the author of a best-seller a celebrity. Publisher and public recalled titles like Margaret Mitchell's *Gone with the Wind* (1937), which had sold five million copies in hardback. Later novels would make claims to greater numbers of sales, but the figures would be inflated by paperback sales, book club editions and, in some cases, foreign editions. In the years immediately before and after World War II, before the paperback became a regular secondary form of publication, hardback best-sellers would stay on the best-seller lists for years. More recently a best-seller rarely lasts for a year on the national lists, and some make a quick trip to the top and drop out of sight within two months.

The stars of the best-seller lists of 1945 were three novels. *Forever Amber* by Kathleen Winsor sold over 1 million copies. It was not a book club choice; it was not distributed to the armed forces; it was not a dividend for a book club. Those sales were over-the-counter bookstore sales, and whatever the author did was news. Her lecture at Symphony Hall in 1946 was referred to as the highlight of the season. *The Robe* by Lloyd Douglas sold over 2.7 million copies, and again, this figure was not inflated by the addition of book club sales or armed forces distribution. That same year *The Black Rose* by Thomas Costain sold over 2 million copies. Like *The Robe* it was a historical novel of a kind which was a staple on the best-seller lists for the next fifteen years.

Though all three might, reread now, seem awkward, overwritten and sentimental, their sales reflect the public hunger for a

good story, especially with a historical setting and moral over-
tones. There was a best-seller of these magnitudes scintillating on
the lists down through 1960: *Marjorie Morningstar* by Herman
Wouk in 1955; *The Last Hurrah* by Edwin O'Connor in 1956; *By
Love Possessed* by James Gould Cozzens in 1957; *Peyton Place* by
Grace Metalious in 1958; *Doctor Zhivago* by Boris Pasternak in
1959; and *Advise and Consent* by Allen Drury in 1960. That was also
the year of the publication of Irving Wallace's *Chapman Report* and
the introduction of high-powered means of publicity intended to
"hype" a book, make it seem more important for some kind of
extraliterary values—its sensational sex, its exposure of some
crime or affair—to blast it on to best-seller lists and make quick
sales. It was also about this year that the republication of the best-
seller in paperback became standard and television became so
well established that it provided an alternative means of enter-
tainment.

Reports on sales of more recent novels like Mario Puzo's *Godfa-
ther* (1969) yield even more startling figures, 12 million, but most
of those sales were in paperback. Sales figures for individual
novels in hardback are rarely released by publishers. It is only
when the novel has begun to sell very well that a publisher may
announce in *Publisher's Weekly* that there are some forty, fifty, or
sixty thousand in print. Thus there was great interest in figures
recently made public by Joni Miller, buyer for hardcover trade
books for the Dalton chain of some 225 department stores based
in Minneapolis but located throughout the mid and far west. All
sales in these stores are fed into a computer. Book sales are identified by individual title to facilitate reordering. According to her
figures, only five percent of hardcover book sales now are for fiction titles. Sales for novels in hardcover are so few by comparison
with sales of hardcover books in other categories that novels
rarely show up on the chain's best-seller lists. So a special low-vol-
ume best-seller list was created for hardcover fiction.

During the summer of 1976, the number one fiction title on that
specially constructed best-seller list had sold 468 copies in all 225
stores during one week. Number ten on the list had sold 60 copies.
In hardcover book sales, nonfiction titles had completely replaced
the top position occupied by novels of a generation ago. Now it is
on the list of general best-sellers—"general" is here preferred to
the term "nonfiction" because many books on the list which were
advertised as factual have proved to be fabrications—that are to

be found the current stars of the publishing world. The general public now buys few hardcover novels by comparison with biographies and is likely to wait for a fiction title to make its appearance in paperback.

Any list of these current best-selling general books is an interesting collection of the substantial and the trivial. There will always be a new biography, as currently, John Toland's *Hitler* which is represented as a careful, possibly definitive study, based on hitherto unconsulted sources. Books like these are candidates for the Pulitzer and other specialized awards. They find their places on library shelves, private and public, and become the authoritative reference sources of the future. Then there will be a book or two on some current fad, like, as of the moment, Sassoon's *Year of Health and Beauty,* the collected ruminations of a hairdresser who has become some kind of celebrity pointing out how various combinations of dieting and grooming can bring what is described as approaching ecstasy. Books on fads like these last but briefly; they become museum pieces. Historians of our taste and culture a generation hence will find much to interest them in the popularity of books on jogging, fiber diets, low-cholesterol diets, all kinds of diets.

Since the big book sales are now among hardback books on this general list, every kind of device is used to get a book on the list. A new diet book will be widely advertised; its author will appear on numerous television shows. For a month, rarely much more, his diet will be the talk of the town, literally, and during that time his book must establish its sales record.

Looking back on lists of best-sellers in *Eighty Years of Best Sellers 1895–1975* by Alice Payne Hackett and James Henry Burke, it is difficult to recover any reason why some book like *Folk Medicine* by D. C. Jarvis became the number two best-seller for 1959, selling over 250,000 copies, or how people could have been so taken by Dr. Herman Taller's *Calories Don't Count* as to make it a 1960 bestseller. Reviewing these lists for the last thirty years, there are obviously certain types of books which recur, cook books, books on housekeeping, biographies, current events. The most persistent category, surprisingly, is what might be called after the first postwar best-seller of this type, "the peace-of-mind book."

Peace of Mind by Joshua Loth Liebman, rabbi of Boston's Temple Israel, was published in the first post–World War II year of 1946 and went on to sell over 1.1 million copies. It appealed to many because it seemed to hold out the promise, that, with its help, many might achieve what Bertrand Russell, in a *Free Man's Worship*, published that same year, had defined as man's greatest triumph, "stability and inner repose in a world of shifting threats and terrifying change."

The genre having been established, *Peace of Mind* was quickly followed the next year by Bishop Fulton Sheen's *Peace of Soul* which achieved sales of only 180,000. Then, in 1952, Norman Vincent Peale followed with *The Power of Positive Thinking* and that went on to surpass *Peace of Mind* with sales of over 2 million copies. All of these books suggested that happiness, stability, adjustment, a cure for whatever vague malaise or feelings of inadequacy people might be experiencing in the postwar world, was available through a little reflection, a little reading, a little self-discipline.

Rereading *Peace of Mind* thirty years later, is a revelation of how much people believed in learning, the power of ideas derived from books to order existence. Basically it is a synthesis, in a style much more leisurely and learned than could be popular today, of a scholar's reading in the classics and the Bible with the addition of what was then still considered the new psychology of Freud.

Rabbi Liebman seems to have anticipated some criticism for his rashness in incorporating so much of the psychiatrist into his orthodox message, so one of the more moving paragraphs in his book reads thus:

"I do not mean to imply that there have not been other pathways to inner serenity than the road now opened by Freud and his successors. It would be absurd, nay impossible, to ignore the great and serene soul of the saints and mystics, the poets and philosophers who achieved peace of mind by other disciplines. As a matter of fact, psychology alone is never enough for man's great adventure—life. Like all other sciences, it formulates no moral goal; it is not a philosophy of life, nor did its pioneers ever intend it to be. It is a key to the temple, not the temple itself. I believe that it must be supplemented by religion, and that only the blended light of these two great beacons will guide individuals and nations through the hazardous channels ahead."

Style and content bespeak an earlier age. The use of alliteration, leisurely balanced clauses, consciously developed metaphors were characteristic of a style more oratorical than direct which was respected a generation ago. The thought represents a continuing dedication to the Renaissance dream that in the explorations of the man of letters, like Shakespeare's Prospero of the *Tempest,* were to be found the wisdom to make life more than transiently meaningful.

Nowhere does the passage of time and the revolution of taste in style and phrasing appear more clearly than in the discussion of love, and what he called the "marital relationship" and "counterfeit forms of love."

"In the marriage relationship also there are many counterfeit forms of love. Whenever you find a husband coercing his wife into surrender of her individuality, or being forced to capitulate to the idiosyncracies and vanities of the mate, there you have a spurious and false form of 'love.' 'Love' is an honorific term, and men and women like to pretend to themselves that they are showing love when as a matter of fact they are displaying possessiveness, jealousy, power, aggression."

With the sentiments, many a liberated woman of the 1970s would completely agree, but the way of expressing it would be considerably different.

In other passages his attitudes are revealed to be considerably different from those of today, and his concerns would now seem to most outmoded. Here he is pointing out how the "penitent," as he calls him, needs counseling; he can't reform entirely without help:

"Incidental release may be obtained through the confessional but the character structure of the penitent is not altered nor are the psychogenic roots of the 'sin' laid bare.

Let me illustrate by an example. A deeply troubled man, thirty-five, married, humbly discloses to his religious counselor that he is carrying on an extra-marital affair. He is very conscious of the pain that he is inflicting on his wife and family. He knows he is doing wrong. The clergyman warns him that adultery is an ugly sin in the sight of God and man, and urges him to bring the affair to a close. The penitent promises to do so, but after a sharp struggle falls back into his old adulterous practice. The advice fails because the spiritual advisor has thrown no light on the cause of this man's sorry plight. He is urged to display more 'will power' and 'stay away' from the other woman. Every minister knows how often these are ineffective councils."

In 1946 adultery was still an "ugly sin" and "penitents" could still be considered to be in a "sorry plight." Peace of mind could not be achieved except by bringing one's way of living into conformity with the expected moral practices of the community.

Though Rabbi Liebman did not believe in the unsupported power of the individual will to enable the individual to achieve self-discipline, Norman Vincent Peale, anticipating the self-help books of the 1970s, did. In *The Power of Positive Thinking,* or *The Positive Principle Today,* he constantly maintains that the individual can achieve wonders if he will but keep trying. Maintain an inspirational, positive attitude at all times, he reiterates; a relentless application of will power and determination will see the individual through to success. To falter, to flirt with negative thoughts, to doubt, these are the ways to failure and self-destruction. This insistence upon the power of the will seems today to argue for a rather simple answer for more complicated problems. But Peale gave many illustrations and anecdotes in which readers might find a message, some possible application to their own cases, and the book inspired many to put its inspirational message into practice.

The equivalent in today's guides to success and equanimity place an equal emphasis on self-determination. Books like *I'm O.K., You're O.K.* by Thomas Harris (1973) stressed the importance of self-assertion if one was to assure his independence and not be victimized by others. This theme became even stronger in Robert Ringer's *Winning through Intimidation* (1975) which is filled with hints on how to get the upper hand on anybody plus any number of pep talks encouraging the seeking of success by running roughshod over anybody in the way. Here success is essentially not being victimized by anyone. A feeling of not being duped, that is the basis of equanimity. One can imagine someone who has had a bad day stopping off during a lunch hour to purchase one of these books, taking it home and resolving that never again will he be anything but determined. Rugged individualism of the last century has deteriorated into the practice of dirty tricks so one can go home nights with the feeling that he took nothing from nobody. What gets done in the interim seems to matter little.

For those who do not wish to fight their way up the ladder of success, who wish to drop out, or for those who value a more peaceful equanimity, the last few years have brought TM, or transcendental meditation. One of the authoritative books on this practice was by Jack Forem and entitled *Transcendental Meditation.* Its subtitle, "Maharishi Mahesh Yogi and the Science of Creative Intelligence," called attention to the Indian guru and self-proclaimed mystic whose visits to this country had done much to popularize this fad. Transcendental meditation was a doctrine of meditation based on Eastern thought which claimed that through its practice an individual could achieve a whole series of benefits: a physiological lowering of high blood pressure, a psychological decrease in anxiety, an increase in mental alertness and awareness. The practice did not require the kinds of prolonged ascetic practices usually required in Eastern, as well as Western religions before the initiate could achieve any kind of trancelike state or euphoria. Rather it was suggested that by a few minutes morning or evening, the repetition of some private mantra or prayer, consciousness would become depersonalized through suspension of memory and some kind of identification with being or nothingness might take place. TM books sold widely; hopefuls signed on for classes in yoga, and many could be seen trying to withdraw and meditate even on commuter trains, seeking that peace of mind that a whole generation had sought but by very different means.

Last year's best-sellers were about TM. This year they are about est, which stands for Eberhard seminar training, named after Werner Erhard who first developed weekend courses which were advertised as guaranteeing the student that they would lead him to acquire "it." What is "it?" According to Robert Hargrove in *Making Life Work,* "it" is the "ability to experience living so that situations you have been trying to change, or have been putting up with, clear up just in the practice of life itself. You get over the feeling that someone out there is doing it to me."

"It" according to Dr. Sheridan Fenwick in *Getting It,* "is to be less anxious, more comfortable in particular kinds of situations, with more self-confidence and more enthusiasm for life." "It" was to be acquired, originally, by signing up for $250 weekend seminars, as some seventy thousand people had, in cities all over the country. Survivors of these seminars were not supposed to reveal, as Dr. Fenwick did, what had taken place. Much of the time of the sessions, as in the book, was taken up by testimonials from those who claimed they had achieved "it." Some had found it easier to talk in public; others achieved greater comfort in all social relations. There seemed to be little difference between the "it" sought by those interested in TM or est, but there was considerable difference between "it" and the peace of mind or soul sought by readers of Rabbi Liebman's or Bishop Sheen's books of a generation earlier.

In the earlier books, there had been much less emphasis on self-assertion and self-realization at the expense of others. In *Peace of Mind,* Rabbi Liebman put it this way: "The science of psychology not only maintains that the drive to give love to the world is an inevitable facet of human nature, but it also insists that man has an innate need for a world of independent human personalities outside the dominion of his own ego." This perception, central to Shakespeare's *King Lear* who also has to discover that he cannot reshape the world to gratify only his own desires for admiration and enjoyment, seems lost to the more recent books. The universal yearning for self-realization which once looked for help through the church and the family has now become completely narcissistic, and the traditions that had animated the older books are now replaced by new slogans and formulas.

A second kind of book which is a perennial on the lists of general best-sellers over the last thirty years has been the rewrite of the history of our times. They are commonly the work of journalists who have had an opportunity to watch the news being made day by day and to write about it. Now they want to sum it up in more permanent terms, give an overall view of what has been happening during their years of observing. Recently we have had Eric Sevareid, for thirty years a nightly commentator on CBS, sum up the century in terms of his autobiography, *Not So Wild a Dream,* and William Shirer, who covered Europe as European correspondent for the *Chicago Tribune,* has done the same with the first volume of his autobiography covering the years from 1904–1930, *Twentieth Century Journey.* These are not autobiographies; their main interest is not in the development of the journalist, but rather in what the journalist saw, what prepared him to see it in his private, prejudiced way. These reviews of their own experiences are intended to help others who have had to stay closer to home not see what they missed but to understand what they had been hearing about only in bits and flashes.

One clear example of this type of book has been Theodore H. White's Making of the President series. Beginning with the campaign of 1960, White, a former *Time* correspondent, has written analyses of what happened in the campaign, what were the crucial decisions, what finally got a candidate elected and defeated the other. It is a kind of journalism which says, in effect, that daily coverage distorts, denies proper perspective. All events are made to seem of equal importance. The reporter who keeps a careful diary, follows the candidate around, but then waits until the votes have been counted can take a long view, bring proportion and understanding to events. The White books on the making of the President have made excellent reading as analyses of the mood of the country during the election year and as summaries of the changes which have come with the passing of the years.

These books share many characteristics with a kind of television program that became very popular in the 1960s, the documentary. The programs undertook to study some single subject—unwed mothers, school integration, homes for the aged — from several points of view. They would present interviews with several subjects, add the opinions of doctors, psychologists, and sociologists, giving the overall impression of a multifaceted study of the subject with no intent to have the last word but rather giving the impression that a complex subject had been presented in a way intended to give viewers the opportunity to make up their own minds. In book form, the studies of the election of a President, the survey of the main movements of a decade were also intended to present complex subjects from multiple points of view. Godfrey Hodgson, for example, after a dozen years as Washington correspondent for the *Times* of London, decided to sum up his impressions of what had been happening in the last ten years in *America in Our Time.* With a great variety of anecdotes and illustrations, he makes us see how the last decade succeeded in destroying two illusions which had been controlling American lives. The disaster of the war in Vietnam and the problems America had been experiencing in its attempt to integrate its educational system had, in Hodgson's opinion, brought home forcibly to Americans that they could no longer delude themselves into believing (1) that "the inequities and injustices of American society were residual and could be abolished without the expenditure of resources on a scale that need not involve any hard choice between priorities," and (2) that "the United States

could use its military power to change the world in conformity
with its wishes and not be itself changed in the process." Hodgson
was pushing for a recognition that "The traditional goals of
absolute freedom and maximum economic abundance will have
to be modified in the more intricate equilibrium of a society that
accepts the limits of human possibility and strives for the greatest
possible measure of justice and equality." Whether many agreed
or disagreed with Hodgson, whether his style was too difficult,
whether his illustrations were not sufficiently numerous, his
America in Our Time did not sell very well, but it did have the kind
of critical reception which frequently distinguished the publication of these documentaries.

The rapid flow of titles on to and then off the best-seller lists has
encouraged the development of fads. If one book of a kind
becomes a best-seller, it is quickly followed by another of the same
type, on the same subject. In the fall of 1976, for no discernible
reason, biographies of men who had made large amounts of
money in oil began to appear, so books on Alfred Hammer, J. Paul
Getty, and H. L. Hunt quickly succeeded each other. Then, just as
suddenly as the biographies of the oil figures began appearing,
they stopped.

Sometimes the fad for a particular book is of longer duration
and reaches enough readers for the book to become a kind of
landmark. Its title serves to define a recognizable type, and the
next book to come along that is similar to it is much more readily
salable. In the 1950s, C. Northcote Parkinson, a professor of history at the University of Singapore, published a study of the way
in which bureaucracies grow. Unrelentingly ironic in style and still
serious in intention, it became widely known for its statement of
Parkinson's Law. Parkinson's Law stated, in effect, that work
expands to fill the space provided. If a bureau or office has been
struggling along with a staff of three, the addition of a fourth will
not result in faster or better work's being done. On the contrary,
the expanded staff may start to accumulate more documents, and
the whole enterprise may become less efficient than it had been
before.

Parkinson's criticism of business organizations from the point
of view of the victims, either the clerk caught up in the machinery
or the taxpayer who has to support the inflated overhead, excited
a group of readers interested in hearing more about the traps in
which they labored. *Parkinson's Law* had created a market for a

kind of book. It was followed by the publication in 1969 of *The Peter Principle* by Lawrence J. Peter and Raymond Hull which traded, in its advertising, on the audience who wanted more of the same. According to the Peter Principle, in a large organization people are always promoted to the level next beyond their abilities to manage, resulting again in waste and inefficiency. So, as Parkinson's Law had become a generally recognized term, invoked to explain why an organization was losing money, so the Peter Principle came to be referred to as an explanation of why a middle manager was incompetent.

In 1970, along came *Up the Organization* by Robert Townsend who had been head of the Avis rent-a-car company. Avis had increased its share of the business by doing something that had not been done in advertising, admitting it was second to the leader in the area, Hertz. But Avis had then gone on to state in its advertisements that, since it was second, it had to try harder. Customers not only tended to believe that was true but also wanted to help the underdog. So Townsend had improved his company's business by unorthodox methods, and his *Up the Organization* was filled with other suggestions similarly revolutionary which he claimed had helped him—and his company—on the way up. Any one of these books, aside from the many chuckles they undoubtedly provided their readers, may also have given some insights into the limitations of big businesses. But they were all faddish books and, unless some other book comes along soon to revive memories of Parkinson's Law or the Peter Principle, they will soon be forgotten.

As a result of the relaxed interpretation of what constituted obscenity in the late 1960s, sex manuals began turning up on the list of nonfiction or general best-sellers. The first was titled *Everything You Always Wanted to Know about Sex but Were Afraid to Ask* by David Reuben, M.D. (1970). With a doctor as author and a title that capitalized on a popular expression which gave the impression the book was an educational effort, it had some protective coloration to shield it from any move by local censors. It was accompanied on the best-seller list for the year by another book which was frankly erotic and made no excuses about it. *The Sensuous Woman* by "J" was a series of detailed suggestions of how a woman might behave like a houri to catch or keep a man about the house. Unreservedly hedonistic, it was a totally uninhibited exposition of postures which a decade before would have been con-

fined to medical textbooks or suggested in the kinds of books
which were on the custom officers' lists. Then came *The Joy of Sex*
by Alex Comfort (1973) and *More Joy: A Lovemaking Companion to
The Joy of Sex* by the same author (1974), and clerks in Lauriat's
bookstore who could remember discussing octavo first editions
and hand-tooled gilded leather covers with customers now found
themselves handing out sex manuals with diagrams as explicit as
the instructions which come with a child's construction set.

The list of general or nonfiction best-sellers published in *Publishers Weekly* for October 25, 1976, contained the mix of titles
which had become typical of such lists over the last decade. There
was the serious attempt at definitive biography, John Toland's
Adolf Hitler, and the ridiculous, the currently faddish grooming
manual, Beverly and Vidal Sassoon's *A Year of Beauty and Health.*
Then there were two Watergate books: *The Right and the Power* by
Leon Jaworski who had been special prosecutor in the congressional investigations, and *The Final Days* by Bob Woodward and
Carl Bernstein, the *Washington Post* reporters who had been the
first to investigate the break-in on the Democratic party headquarters in the Watergate apartment complex which had led to
the resignation of President Nixon.

Then there was the self-help book, *Your Erroneous Zones* by Dr.
Wayne W. Dyer, which was to help the unsuccessful to overcome
their handicaps, and the humor book by Erma Bombeck, *The
Grass Is Always Greener over the Septic Tank,* a collection of wry essays
on the problems of suburban living.

The two distinctive books on the list were Alex Haley's *Roots,* the
summary of a black man's ten-year search for his ancestors which
had carried him all the way back to an African village, and *Passages*
by Gail Sheehy, a study of the crises emotional and financial in
adult life. *Roots* stayed on the best-seller list for a year and
encouraged the development of a national fad which had many
people taking up a search for their ancestors. *Passages* represented a kind of documentary study of the problems of middle
age, pretentious in parts with its use of sociological and psychological jargon, interesting in its anecdotage, but short-lived.
Interestingly, both these books became the subjects of law suits by
authors claiming that their materials had been incorporated into
them without their receiving recognition.

A Man Called Intrepid by William Stevenson, the story of a British
agent operating out of the United States during World War II,

was number eight on the list and not receiving much attention. It was a good story, certainly not all history, and a good illustration of why books on the list should not be called nonfiction because there were passages in it more imagined than documented. *Intrepid* received a lot of word-of-mouth recommendation, and soon it was one of the most popular books locally. It was a proof that though intense advertising campaigns could put a book like *Roots*, dubious as it might be in retrospect, at the top of the list, readers could still influence the course of sales by their personal recommendations. What was equally interesting, studying that list, was how little choice there was for readers, either in variety of subject or quality of style. At this time of year, heading into the Christmas sales season, the publishers had their best books out, and there wasn't a one that would still be talked about a generation hence except as an index to changing tastes in postwar Boston.

8

From *How to Read a Book* to How to Read a Best-Seller List

Had full documentation on the Aristotle family survived, it is not unlikely that it would contain some reference to father Nichomachus's doubts about the way his son was being taught. A physician, some of his calls upon his patients around Athens would have taken him by the Lyceum where he must have noticed the way Plato had his students sitting about him asking and answering questions. To a conventional citizen of Athens, certain questions must certainly have come to mind. Whatever happened to the training in oratory? Aren't the students taught how to compose, memorize, and deliver speeches anymore? What is wrong with the way Aeschines used to train his students to be effective in speaking before the assembly of citizens?

And so it has been from the beginning with each generation questioning the value of the education the next seems to be receiving, asking why the curriculum has changed, why discipline has been relaxed, why standards have been reduced. Currently, parental worry seems focused on why Johnny is not being taught to write properly. A generation ago, the magazines were publishing articles reflecting a national concern with why Johnny couldn't read.

In the *Atlantic Monthly* for 1939, professor James Mursell of Columbia University was credited with an essay entitled, "The Failure of the Schools," which would be a safe title for an article during any year. His study of the current reading problem showed that "up to the fifth and sixth grade, reading, on the whole, is effectively taught and well-learned. To that level we find a steady and general improvement, but beyond it the curves flatten out to a dead level." His main concern, however, was with the high school graduate for, upon his ability to read persuasive prose, to analyze arguments directed at him, depended his ability to function effectively as a citizen. It was there that professor Mursell thought the schools had failed.

> The average high-school graduate has done a great deal of reading and if he goes on to college he will do a great deal more; but he is likely to be a poor and incompetent reader. He can follow a simple piece of fiction and enjoy it. But put him up against a closely written exposition, a carefully and economically stated argument, or a passage requiring critical consideration, and he is at a loss. It has been shown, for instance, that the average high-school student is amazingly inept at indicating the central thought of a passage, or the levels of emphasis and subordination in an argument or exposition.

With this assessment of forty years ago, many college teachers today would still agree. Students are still much better at reading and interpreting simple narrative than they are at analyzing, summarizing, and evaluating any kind of argumentative exposition. Today we seem less concerned about it than parents and professors were a generation ago.

Thus there was a ready-made market for Mortimer Adler's *How to Read a Book* which was published first in 1940 and quickly became the second best-selling title of the year. The book became a classic and was widely read and used in Great Books Seminars for a number of years. When it was reissued in 1972, with extensive revisions to provide a discussion of the speed reading courses which were then the fad, there was nowhere near the same popular response as had greeted its first appearance. *How to Read a Book* represents an important landmark in our changing culture. First, it was a popularization, in the best sense of the word, of the skills of the classical trivium, the arts of grammar, rhetoric, and logic, which were no longer being studied as they had for centuries by every student who pretended to a liberal education. Second, it provided a methodology for the study of the world's great books toward which many still looked for wisdom in the solution of personal and national problems. Third, it was an illustration of a critical approach which judged a work on the basis of the extent to which it realized its intention and not on the basis of whether the critic agreed with its content. Though nothing more than an adaptation of Aristotelian principles, Adler's book struck the country as novel, and its application in the teaching of literature courses at the University of Chicago was so different that its practitioners were tagged as "New Critics."

To become a proper citizen of his democracy, the Athenian lad was sent to the pedagogue to learn the arts of the trivium: grammar, to become familiar with the rules governing the clear speaking of his language; logic, to learn the proper and fallacious forms of arguments; and rhetoric, to recognize the schemes and tropes used by orators to sway their audiences so they themselves could use them when they rose to speak in the assembly. Democratic forms of government, then as well as now, were predicated upon the ability of their citizens to evaluate proposed policies and to be able to take part in the public deliberations that controlled their acceptance or rejection.

To use a word that has become very popular in the last decade, democracies assume a citizen's ability to take part in a "dialogue." The guarantees of freedom of speech are necessary if everyone, and every idea, is to have a chance to be heard. In *How to Read a Book,* Mortimer Adler took principles from all three arts of the trivium and wove them together in a collection intended to show the reader how to engage in a dialogue with a book. By following Adler's suggestions, the reader learned how to summarize a book, to isolate its main propositions, how to test their supporting arguments, how to evaluate their interrelations, how, finally, to proceed to a determination of whether he agreed with the book. What he learned to do with a book could, presumably, be extended to other forms of presentation used in public debate. In the end he not only knew what he thought, but why and how to go about persuading others to a similar point of view.

The reader's first responsibility in undertaking to understand properly according to Mortimer Adler in *How to Read a Book* is stated this way at the conclusion of a section entitled, "The First Stage of Analytical Reading": "Classify the book according to kind and subject matter." This is exactly what Aristotle did in his *Poetics* when he set out to analyze tragedy, identify the kind of thing we are going to talk about. Make sure we agree that we are studying the same species of thing. From his physician father, Aristotle learned some of the basic principles a good zoologist should follow, which is what he was, first and foremost. So the first three chapters of the *Poetics* are devoted to defining the kind of animal he is going to study. The reader should begin by making sure that

he knows what kind of book he is about to read so he won't expect
from a novel what an epic should do or from a comedy what an
essay should seek to accomplish. This does not mean that he must
discover this right on the first page, but it is the reader's responsibility to determine what sort of thing he is reading as soon as he
can and not to seek to derive from the book what it was never
intended to accomplish.

The second stage the reader should attempt to achieve is to
"state what the whole book is about with the utmost brevity." Again
this is not to be achieved upon reading the first page or the first act
or the first chapter. It can only be attempted after reading the
work in its entirety and the summary can then be offered tenta-
tively as a hypothesis. Mark Van Doren, for many years professor
of English at Columbia and respected lecturer on Shakespeare,
has been credited with offering to recommend anyone who could
state in a single sentence the purpose of Shakespeare's *King Lear*
for immediate graduation. Van Doren, like Mortimer Adler was a
product of John Erskine's Great Books courses at Columbia in the
1920s, and they, not the later courses at the University of Chicago
as is commonly supposed, were the beginnings of the movement.
It is also worth noting here that what the reader should try to state
with as much brevity as possible is the purpose the work seems
intended to achieve, not the purpose the author of the work may
have declared he intended. Writers sometimes write better than
they intend; sometimes they write worse, and sometimes, if we are
to believe Freud or Jung, their unconscious uses them as an inter-
mediary for messages whose import they may only barely perceive.

The third stage is to "enumerate the book's major parts in their
order and relation, and outline these parts as you have outlined
the whole." Any time a reader can state succinctly the purpose ful-
filled by the book and then demonstrate the way in which each of
the parts of the book makes a contribution to the realization of
that purpose, he can be said to know the book as a whole and in its
parts. In the *Poetics,* Aristotle was constantly arguing that the tragedy that is unified, the tragedy wherein every part contributes to
the realization of the purpose of the whole, the creation of pity
and fear and the purgation thereof, was the best kind of tragedy.
Stated baldly, classifying the book, defining its purpose, and identifying its parts do not seem too difficult. But actually only careful

reading, repeated testing of suggested definitions by constant reference to the book, can result in statements that will stand up.

When reading expository prose like newspaper editorials, essays in magazines, chapters in some book analyzing what's wrong with us today, the intent of the work may be easier to summarize than when grappling with a serious novel. In a novel, the thrust of the work may only gradually become clear, and the interrelationship of parts may be very difficult to perceive until after repeated readings. In an essay on current matters, the writer usually gets around to stating the proposition which he is out to demonstrate. Like a lawyer defending a client, he comes right out and says that he is going to prove the accused innocent. So in reading an essay or book, first find the proposition, and that will go a long way toward indicating the overall purpose of the work.

The second step in reading argumentative materials is to find the reasons offered in support of the proposition, the "because" clauses which, in the writer's opinion, prove what he is defending. Sometimes a reader following this procedure will be surprised to discover that there is no supporting reason, no because clause. All the writer has done, figuratively speaking, is to thump the table, shout, repeat his proposition in other words, jump up and down insisting that he is right, but he has not offered the reflective reason a single fact, similar situation, indicated what results might be expected to make him agree. The responsible reader who will not accept a proposition or adopt a proposed course of action on somebody else's mere say-so gets in the habit of "briefing" an essay he is reading. He reduces it to a series of propositions and their supporting reasons. When there are no reasons, there is no basis for agreeing with the writer unless the reader just wants to.

The traditional training in rhetoric always referred to the fallacy of gratuitous assertion: "Whatever is gratuitously asserted can be gratuitously denied." In other words, don't waste your time proving someone wrong if he hasn't given you a single reason for believing him right. Without a reason to support a position, a writer has only his vanity to lead him to suppose he will be listened to. So much of classical rhetoric was devoted to teaching the student how to draw up enthymemes. An enthymeme is a proposition and its supporting reason. A series of enthymemes constitutes a brief. A lawyer with a brief has a series of enthymemes which, he is convinced, when taken together make his case. A carefully written book can be "debriefed," the skeleton of supporting arguments recovered by the reader. Upon the ability of readers to read in this fashion, or, better still, upon the habit of readers to do this with all serious arguments advanced for their consideration, depends the existence of an informed and responsible citizenry.

The same skill or habit should also be brought to bear in the reading of book reviews, or drama reviews, or reviews of any of the arts. Any review is, after all, an argument advanced by a critic in support of his judgment of a novel or a symphony—or whatever. The minimum a reader of a review should expect is an enthymeme, the proposition saying in effect, "This is a good piece or bad piece of work," and the reason "because it is well constructed or badly executed." What the reader of a review wants to know is why he should agree with the reviewer. Any person can be left to enjoy his personal reaction to a work of art, but he can hardly expect everyone else to share his ecstasy unless he points to reasons that others can recognize or experience for themselves. The difficulty with much that passes for criticism currently is that it lacks a clearly formulated proposition, and supporting reasons, if they are proferred, are frequently irrelevant.

In *The Critics,* Lehman Engel, a major force in the theater as director, award-winning composer, and conductor, reviewed the people who had been reviewing his efforts for the previous forty years. Of Clive Barnes, a *New York Times* reviewer, he concluded: "Barnes' enthusiasm and over-extended activity produced cavalier reviews that have harmed the theater." By "cavalier" here, he seems to have meant "off-the-cuff," "unsupported." Of John Simon, another critic, he had this estimate: "Since he is innately brilliant, it is a pity that he should find it necessary to resort to making personal quips to someone else's indefensible embarrassment." Criticism that is supported by objective reasons is always respected, even if the reader may not, finally, agree with it. Walter Kerr, for many years chief critic for the *New York Times,* has always been respected because, according to Engel, "What Kerr does superbly is draw the reader into the experience that he had...His conclusions are substantiated and clearly expressed...The theatergoer will find in Kerr's presentation an unbiased fairness and a reasonable and developed point of view." The key words and phrases in that evaluation are: "conclusions," "substantiated," the opposite of "cavalier," and "reasonable and developed point of view," the opposite of "personal quips" leading to someone else's embarrassment. Critical judgments are reasonable or substantiated or objective, the adjectives are not entirely synonymous, but they share the least common denominator of meaning the opposite of subjective, when they are supported by what students will accept in response to their demand to, "Give me an instance." In all classes, from mathematics through foreign languages, there is nothing that will help a student to understand more than to give him an instance. Also giving an instance provides the student—or the reader—with an opportunity to examine a proposition out in the open, as something supported by more than a subjective feeling.

So, in a respectable piece of criticism, the proposition is supported by reasons. There are, very largely speaking, two general areas from which reasons supporting a favorable or critical judgment of a work may be drawn: its subject matter and its form. According to the *Phaedrus* of Plato, the most important single element determining the value of a piece is whether it tells the truth. According to Aristotle in the *Poetics,* the most important single element determining whether a piece is a good piece of work is the unity of its form.

As long as there was a large body of readers who shared common assumptions about the source of truth, proper behavior, and the basis of morality, criticism of literature could be Platonic, criticism of content. As long as there was in Boston a population to support the *Evening Transcript* and what it stood for, criticism could appeal to commonly held community standards. When that group had become fragmented, when there were many smaller groups, none of which constituted a majority, then criticism had to become criticism of form, of structure, of construction. Poems and novels were evaluated no more from the point of view of the integrity of their ideas—Who now had the pipeline to God?—but from the point of view of their integrity of form.

This was the so-called New Criticism, the criticism which many associated with the University of Chicago, a kind of criticism which was taught implicitly and encouraged explicitly by Adler's *How to Read a Book.* The new strategy for the critic, as weekend supplement essayist or classroom performer, was to discuss the relations of the parts to the whole, of the stanzas to the ode, not the logic of the poet's ideas. Critics like Malcolm Brinnin of Boston University, interested in something more than tesselation, attacked this position in a "Defence of the Relevance of Sentimentality." "In recent history," he said, "we have been asked to think of poems and novels not as living documents or *cris-de-coeurs*, but as nice structures, symbolic choreographies, models of confusion and so on. The poem, *qua* poem, and the novel, *qua* novel, we were told should ideally exhibit an internal structure and reticulum of ideas."

The New Criticism, in his opinion, "gave rein to a whole generation of instructors whose performances were awesome. These were the linguistic technicians who could, in a mere thirty minutes, dismantle an epic and, in the next twenty minutes, put it together again with not even one pathetic fallacy left over to clean up. These were the academic prodigies who could take some little old Model T of a poem, clean its spark plugs, drain its crankcase, pack its wheelbases, and have it back on the road twenty seconds before the eleven o'clock bell rang."

There was a lot of good and bad to this application of the heuristic methodologies to general criticism. On the good side, it set the whole post–World War II generation of students to reading poems and novels instead of listening to lectures about the personalities of the poets and novelists who wrote them. The pre–World War II college survey had been conducted in large classrooms with hundreds listening to lecturers passing on tea-table gossip about Byron or Shelley or Yeats. This had now been replaced by smaller classes whose members sat with a text of Byron or Shelley or Yeats in front of them and who were quizzed by an instructor to try to make them see what the poet had been trying to say. They were encouraged to hypothecate some integrating idea, thereby developing their critical perceptions as well as willingness to defend their insights. They were forced to defend, with reasons from the text, their interpretations. They were being taught what to look for in a book and how to support what, in their opinion, they thought they had found.

What was bad about this approach to the teaching and criticism of literature was the impression it conveyed that all that mattered was construction and technique. Since students could easily conclude that what was said was not as important as how it was said, the fiery creative spirit seemed less important than the careful, meticulous builder. The university professors who could take a poem apart and put it back together in a regular fifty-minute class period, when they became involved in reviewing for the *New York*

Times or the *New York Review of Books* concentrated on the explication of points of view, technical competence, time sequences. Writers looked for approval of their voice, their tone, other qualities than their prejudices, their vigor in the defence of their positions. Theatrical producer Merrick was widely quoted as saying that what the theater of the seventies needed was a young person with fire in his guts and a determination to be heard.

In a talk at the Breadloaf Writers' Conference in August 1974, Seymour Epstein, a Random House editor and one of the founding fathers of the *New York Review of Books* discussed this feeling of many young writers that their ideas never got a hearing. He thought that concern with technique was a substitute for concern with substance and acknowledged that books chosen for major spots in book review media were frequently chosen because they were structurally interesting. Writers abroad, it seemed to him, had tended to eschew realism, or other commitments, when such a commitment would have been tantamount to shutting themselves off from a large section of a possibly large audience. Since writers who are not reviewed are never widely read, American authors began to concentrate on the devices and tricks likely to land them on the front pages of the book review sections. The post–World War II novelists were successes not because they were learned, illuminated a problem, or had a beautiful style. They were "interesting" and "technically accomplished."

At the opening of *Wickford Point,* John Marquand introduces his readers to Allan Southby, the Harvard tutor who has written a pretentious book on American civilization entitled *The Transcendent Curve.* Many people bought it because the title implied so much, the maroon binding bespoke taste and culture. Marquand then made this comment: *"The Transcendent Curve* did, however, get him nearly everywhere he wanted to go, because he knew how to use that book, and its immense success in no wise turned his head from what he wanted: he wanted to be a man of letters, a figure more austere and just a trifle more formal than Professor Phelps of Yale."

Today it is difficult to think of someone who might be generally accepted as a man of letters. The term has lost much of its meaning and possibly all of its aura. This is the age of the specialist; yesterday was the day of the humanist, the all-around scholar whose pronouncements were supposed to sum up a tradition and illuminate a problem against the background of ideas in which all believed. Locally Harvard boasted of an Irving Babbitt and a George Santayana who spoke and wrote with an authority that only a widespread belief in the book and humanism could support.

Writing of the man of letters in *Hero and Hero Worship* Thomas Carlyle claimed that he was "our most important modern person." He was the generalist, the scholar humanist, who most likely taught at a university, wrote very well, and was widely respected. John Gross, currently editor of the London *Times Literary Supplement* and author of *The Rise and Fall of the Man of Letters* (1969), traces the decline of the term, "man of letters," to the period after World War I. The specialist then came to be admired, and the man of letters seemed to pretend to more than he could grasp. Gross, who was responsible for introducing the signed review into the pages of the *Times Literary Supplement,* admits that he searches in vain for the man of letters to write reviews. He finds himself using specialists who always feel obliged to point to some minor omission in a book to demonstrate that they know more than the author whom they are reviewing. There is a great temptation for an editor to have a novel with an anthropologist as hero or with a setting in a primitive society reviewed by an anthropologist who proceeds to point to all the inaccurate details and to disregard the main point of the book. If the review is savage enough, it may be talked about more than the book it supposedly discussed. Sometimes it seems that Carlyle's fears, expressed in an essay on reviewers and reviewing in the *Edinburgh Review* of 1831, have come all too true. Even back then, Carlyle was concerned about the importance which was being increasingly attached to reviewing. "Far be it from us," he wrote, "to disparage our own craft, whereby we have our living! Only we must note these things: that reviewing spreads with strange vigor; that such a man as Byron reckons the reviewer and the poet equal; that at the last Leipzig Fair, there was advertised a Review of Reviews. By and by it will be found that all literature has become one boundless self-devouring review."

In a hundred fifty years, Carlyle has not proved to be a complete prophet, not quite. There are several review media that are very active, but not all are equal by any means in their impact on the public and their determination of public taste. Many of them seem less interested in reaching out for that broad public than in writing for a group of the like-minded.

In *The End of Intelligent Writing,* Richard Kostelanetz argues that, since its founding in 1963, reviews in the *New York Review of Books* are not so much criticisms or "judgments of perception but gestures of social solidarity." He develops a case intended to demonstrate that the *Review* is unusually sympathetic to books published by Random House and calls attention to the involvement of Jacob Epstein, a Random House editor, in the founding of the *Review* and the presence of his wife on the editorial board. He documents his case by claiming that four out of the five most frequently featured poets in the *New York Review* are poets whose books have been published by Vintage Books, an imprint with which Jacob Epstein is involved, and that sixteen of the twenty-three featured essayists are Random House authors.

In the years immediately following World War II, the most readily identifiable group of writers were the Southern fugitives: Allan Tate, Cleanth Brooks, Robert Penn Warren, John Crowe Ransom, Robert Heilman. They had all taught at southern universities, shared similar interpretations of history which looked back on the antebellum South as the flowering of American humanistic culture, and tended to publish in the same magazines, for example, the *Sewanee Review.* They were in demand as visiting lecturers at universities. Brooks and Warren's anthology, *Understanding Poetry,* with its emphasis on textual analysis, was widely used and influenced the teaching of literature all over the country. They supported one another for appointments and furthered each other's publications. But they were never successful in conquering the national media as reviewers and, with the exception of Robert Penn Warren, who became nationally known as a novelist for his *All the King's Men,* they had their influence in narrower circles as poets and critics.

"In the years of the fifties," Kostelanetz writes in *The End of Intelligent Writing,* "the same pattern as had been followed by the Southern Fugitives of insurgence was duplicated by another well-organized literary minority, the Jewish-American writers." The pattern followed by the Southern writers and the Jewish-American group was to test previous writers according to their beliefs and seek a revision of the past. They would constantly invoke the names of their models and neglect the others in a "regular phalanx of magazines ranging from quarterlies through a monthly through the literary pages of a weekly." The New York crowd, according to Kostelanetz, was better organized than the Southern group, for they have "a force of ambitious sometime students and proteges willing to undertake minor tasks for which the elders no longer had the time, guts or energy; allies in the major reviewing media; cooperative conduits in New York publishing; anthologies that would place their names beside the acknowledged champs; and the attempt to make one of their number into the foremost novelist of his time (the Saul-Bellow-shall-be-our-greatest-writer-or-bust movement) which so far conquered one international prize and has at least one to go. They emphasized not poetry and extended critical essays like their predecessors but fiction and book reviews, which are inherently more popular forms."

The group was unquestionably successful—Saul Bellow was awarded the Noble Prize for Literature in 1976—and the pattern they have established continues today. The New York review media, the *New York Times Book Review* and the *New York Review of Books,* founded while the *New York Times* was out on strike in 1963, have come to dominate the field. There are other book review sections across the country, but they are not as widely read, nor are they used as commonly by public librarians as guides to their purchasing. Without a review in either of the New York media, a book passes relatively unnoticed. Without major review space in the *New York Times Book Review,* a novel has little chance of becoming a national best-seller. It is here that a novel can get its major "hype," be reviewed in highly quotable terms—"tremendous," "shocking," "bold," "earthy"—which will then be splashed across large advertisements in succeeding weeks supporting the initial thrust toward notoriety received from the review.

Review space in all the various outlets reviewing books, whether they be quarterlies, monthlies, or national weeklies, is tight. Facts about how much space is available, who decides how it is to be allocated, and what determines the allocation are as difficult to come by as hard figures from publishers stating exactly how many copies of a novel were printed and how many were sold, or equally hard figures from bookstores stating how many copies of a specific title were sold.

At a meeting of the Publishers' Publicity Association, a group of directors of publicity for the various publishers, in New York in February 1979, the staff of the *New York Times Book Review* let its hair down and appealed for some understanding from the publicity representatives of the problems of the editors of the book review. Harvey Shapiro, editor of the *New York Times Book Review* gave out as the "official figure" of books received for review in the preceding year as 38,000. It would have been 40,000 if it were to include books from small presses and self-published titles. Of the total number of books received, 2,300 were reviewed, about six percent. This was broken down into the following categories: fiction and poetry, 539; nonfiction, 845; paperbacks, 590; children's books, 319.

Richard Locke, deputy editor of the *Times Book Review* estimated that the 1.5 million copies of the *Review* printed reached about four million readers. So any one can see how important it is to be reviewed in the *Times Book Review,* and all should bear in mind that of the 2,300 books reviewed only a very few get the star treatment: a review starting on the front page with some kind of illustration and, most likely, some accompanying interview with the author. That kind of treatment turns a book into a celebrity of the book world and practically ensures its eventual best-seller status. Among all those novels and collections of poems, there were many which received only a couple of sentences, enough to be counted, to inflate and distort the figures. Eden Ross Lipson, an editor of the *Times Book Review,* spoke volumes when he urged publicists for the various publishers to "hold off on your duty or obligation calls; please call when you are expressing a serious opinion about a book's value." One can only begin to imagine the number of calls and the other forms of recommendation aimed at the decision makers to secure for a book that all important review space.

A book accorded major review space and receiving a favorable review is also assured space on the shelves of bookstores. Books are now merchandised like breakfast cereals in a supermarket. Established products are guaranteed shelf space. New products are granted a test period. If they don't sell, they are returned to the manufacturer within a set period in order to qualify for the return of their discounted cost. New products which are guaranteed the support of an extensive advertising program are granted display space. The first novel without an advertising budget, with practically zero chance of being reviewed in a noticeable fashion, is literally condemned to external darkness and a minimum readership.

Successful sales win a place for the book on the best-seller lists, and that is not only a form of continuing, free advertising but also a means of prolonging the book's sales. Many people looking for a book to read for themselves or as a gift for a friend will consult the best-seller list. Librarians commonly post these lists, especially the list concocted by the *New York Times,* in prominent places. Infrequent readers, unfamiliar with the names of the authors on a current list nevertheless feel that any title on the list is probably a better bet as a good "read" than some book they might pick out for themselves.

Best-sellers therefore become celebrities of the book world. What is a celebrity? A celebrity is any person who manages to get himself or herself written about. Many of the celebrities who are perennials on television interview programs are not particularly distinguished for any talent, but they may have had an interesting love affair which caught some journalist's attention. They were written about. Now they are talked about. The fact that a book is a celebrity says nothing of its quality, only of its good fortune.

Stories demonstrating the unreliability of best-seller lists are common property in the book trade. Publishers have been puzzled to notice that one of their titles was supposedly a best-seller when they were not shipping any of the titles from their warehouse. The answer proved to be a friend of the author who owned two bookstores and who reported his friend's book as his best-seller week after week. In November 1975, *Esquire* magazine published the second of three projected excerpts from a forthcoming novel by Truman Capote, *Answered Prayers.* People began asking for the unpublished novel, and at least two bookstores reported it as their best-seller.

As publishers will rarely state exactly how many copies of a novel have been sold, so bookstores rarely keep exact records of how many copies of each of the titles they have on hand they sold the previous week. When a newspaper, local or national, or a magazine like *Time* or *Publishers Weekly,* calls to obtain the raw data which will go into a best-seller list, the bookstore does not report specific number of sales but rather reports a list of ten or fifteen titles in an order chosen by whoever is reporting the list. The clerk answering the phone may give as the number one best-seller the title he thinks he sold the most of last week, or the title of an author he likes, or he may look around the floor and see which stacks have diminished the most. He may, if hurried, even read off last week's best-seller list, or, if anxious about the slow sales of a title the store overbought, give that title to encourage sales.

Newspapers do not reveal the names of the stores they call in order to construct their lists. Ray Walters of the *New York Times* claimed, in a story on best-seller lists published by the *Los Angeles Times* on Friday, September 17, 1976, that the *Times* called some two hundred fifty bookstores to make up its list. (Since then the *New York Times* has computerized its data collecting and claims to include reports from over one thousand stores in its weekly best-seller list.) What was never revealed was the location of these stores. Most are undoubtedly metropolitan and few are of the small town card-shop variety. Furthermore, never made clear is how the reports from the various stores are weighted. Is the number one best-seller from a major outlet, a Fifth Avenue Brentano's, counted the same as the number one best-seller from a small bookstore on Cape Cod?

Most readers are unaware how few copies of a book must be sold each week to make it a store's best-seller. Local bookstores will frequently sell only three to five copies of a book that will rank on the top ten of a best-seller list. In its story on best-seller lists, the *Los Angeles Times* reports several incidents where an author, learning what stores reported their sales to national best-seller lists, had their friends buy several copies in each store–in one case ten copies in seven stores–and the next week they were number five on the *New York Times* best-seller list. Motion picture studios have been aware of this possibility for some years, and producer Robert Evans admits that "a buy like that was made" for *Love Story* when he was executive vice-president of Paramount Studios. Such programs may cost a studio, it has been estimated, between ten thousand and twenty thousand dollars, but it is a sound investment. Bookstores claim they can spot the beginnings of such a campaign. They suddenly find themselves handed new ten dollar bills at lunchtime for a particular title, the money doled out to secretaries and workers by the studio. For the cost of a full-page advertisement in a national medium, the studio can achieve what the advertisement can't do by itself. Though the technique of concentrated buying in the right stores can get a book on best-seller lists, keeping it there is something else again. Unless the book catches on, its stay on the lists will be brief and may not do the studios intending to bring it out as a movie much good.

So although best-seller lists are great sales tools for booksellers and for publishers whose titles manage to make the list, most editors, either of book sections or of the journals which carry them, who are familiar with their weaknesses would just as soon get rid of them. But, since the public continues to be interested in celebrities, to read the lists like racing forms, each week noting who is first, how many weeks he has been up there, editors keep on printing them. In some instances, as in the *New York Times* and *Time* magazine, the best-seller lists are supplemented by lists of editors' recommendations. These commonly contain titles of books that have not been reported as best-sellers but which, in the opinion of editors and reviewers, are at least as important and probably more significant and better written. It is not unusual for the books recognized by national or international prizes at the end of the year never to have made a best-seller list. Readers who allow themselves to be guided by the lists are similar to television viewers who get their news from the interview shows.

Thirty years after the last successful banning of a book in Boston, readers undoubtedly enjoy a greater freedom in their choice of books. No longer can a small group, representing but a segment of the community taste, prevent the general circulation of a book that they find offensive. With the coming of the greater freedom of the last thirty years has come a greater responsibility. The reader is now responsible for all his choices. No longer can it be said, as it was at the time of the banning of *Strange Fruit*, that greater freedom for the artist would result in better books for the public. It has resulted in more, not necessarily better, books. With the increased numbers competing for attention in the marketplace, sophisticated marketing techniques have been developed, and the reader without critical habits will be taken in by the constant "hyping," overpraising of books and the manipulation of opinions. The last thirty years have seen great changes in public taste in Boston. Taste never stands still, but taste which is unexamined is susceptible to the most immediate pressures. Taste, like style, is to be acquired only slowly, reflectively. That is the only way of ensuring the survival of the best.